THE 21 IRREFUTABLE
LAWS OF LEADERSHIP

Follow Them and People
Will Follow You

JOHN C. MAXWELL

THOMAS NELSON PUBLISHERS
Nashville

Published in Nashville, Tennessee, by Thomas Nelson, Inc.

Scripture quotations noted CEV are from THE CONTEMPORARY EN-GLISH VERSION. Copyright © 1991 by the American Bible Society. Used by permission.

Library of Congress Cataloging-in-Publication Data

Maxwell, John C., 1947–
    The 21 irrefutable laws of leadership : follow them and people will follow you / John C. Maxwell.
        p.   cm.
    ISBN 0-7852-7034-5
    1. Leadership. 2. Industrial management. I. Title.
HD57.7.M3937   1998
658.4'092—dc21

                                                                98-8365
                                                                CIP

Printed in the United States of America.

56 57 PHX 04

PRAISE FOR
THE 21 IRREFUTABLE LAWS OF LEADERSHIP

John Maxwell is a leader who has graciously shared his secrets with the rest of us. Break these 21 laws of leadership at your own peril. They truly are the foundation upon which all of us, no matter our position, can build a life, a purpose, and a mission.

STEPHEN ARTERBURN
FOUNDER AND CHAIRMAN, NEW LIFE CLINICS

John Maxwell has bridged the gap between secular business approaches and Bible-based principles with a winning formula for successful leadership. This book will truly inspire you to give your best efforts to the people you lead.

ANNE BEILER
FOUNDER, AUNTIE ANNE'S HAND-ROLLED SOFT PRETZELS

An irrefutable must-read on leadership that is a simple and powerful list of guidelines to help build leadership in many arenas.

S. TRUETT CATHY
FOUNDER AND CHAIRMAN, CHICK-FIL-A, INC.

The messenger is the message. *The 21 Irrefutable Laws of Leadership* is more than a book—John Maxwell allows you an in-depth view of himself, the messenger. The principles in this book are much more than mere theoretical constructs; they leap off the pages due to their relevance and practicality. Anyone can tell you *what* to do; John takes you beyond that and shows you the *how* of leadership. Why another book on leadership? Two specific reasons—first, this book, while based on sound biblical principles, shows the secularist the relevance of these eternal laws. Second, this book allows the leader-reader to utilize it as a premium tool in mentoring other leaders. Each stand-alone chapter is complete in its message. John has most certainly made a contribution to the kingdom of God through this book as well as to those outside the world of professed Christianity—it's the Word in the marketplace.

DR. SAMUEL R. CHAND
PRESIDENT, BEULAH HEIGHTS BIBLE COLLEGE, ATLANTA, GA

The marketplace is cluttered with books and products about leadership. But writing about leadership doesn't make one an expert on leadership. Being a leader makes one an expert on leadership. John Maxwell is a proven leader and builder. He's also not afraid to admit to having made mistakes, and the reader benefits from lessons learned from those mistakes. *The 21 Irrefutable Laws of Leadership* provides a good blueprint for success as a leader and a barometer for gauging leadership ability.

MARK DeMOSS
PRESIDENT, THE DeMOSS GROUP, INC.

John Maxwell's latest book is a treasure chest full of insight on key principles of effective leadership. Within these pages, you'll find irrefutable wisdom, and Maxwell illustrates the 21 laws through interesting, real-life stories and personal anecdotes. The ideas presented in this book are simple, clear, and easy to grasp . . . yet profound! It's an enjoyable, easy-to-read book that is educational yet entertaining. Whether you are a recent graduate just beginning your career, or a seasoned executive, this book is worth reading . . . and keeping at hand as a leadership reference guide.

TOM WHATLEY
PRESIDENT, U.S. SALES, MARY KAY, INC.

Dr. Maxwell has established, for anyone interested in touching others' lives, a 21-point map to leading, influencing, and just better living. He does this with interesting, engaging stories. I couldn't put this book down.

DR. P. KEVIN ELKO
CORPORATE CONSULTANT AND PERFORMANCE CONSULTANT
TO THE PITTSBURGH STEELERS

We live in an age of "special effects" leadership techniques, where show holds away over substance. There is certainly no dearth of people telling us how to lead. Yet our nation and its institutions are crying out for leaders. John Maxwell, with his customary insight, depth of experience, and entertaining style shows us the true path to leadership through the application of timeless principles supported by the bedrock of personal character. This is a must read for any individual who seriously desires to become an effective leader.

EDWARD C. EMMA
PRESIDENT & COO, JOCKEY INTERNATIONAL, INC.

My good friend John Maxwell has placed the subject of leadership on a low enough shelf for all existing and potential leaders to partake of its fruit and enjoy its benefits. This is must reading for all who wish to understand and emulate authentic leadership.

DR. TONY EVANS

This fascinating brainchild of John's is a composite of all he has personally learned about leadership. Each chapter is expressed simply and succinctly, accompanied by the encouraging words that the laws of leadership can be learned. What a terrific benefit to all who want to excel in their role as leaders.

BARBARA HAMMOND
PRESIDENT, HOME INTERIORS & GIFTS, INC.

Absolutely one of the finest readings on leadership and success principles that I've ever read. It has to go on the top shelf of your study library—right after you've put these laws in use for yourself.

B. LEE HARRISON JR.
PRESIDENT AND FOUNDER, NORTH FLORIDA FINANCIAL CORPORATION

John's sensitivity, his insight into human nature, and his fidelity to our Creator's timeless success principles blend to bring both a practical functionality and a value-based integrity to his work. His leadership ideas are masterful because his life and thoughts are Master-full.

JACK W. HAYFORD, D.LIT.
SENIOR PASTOR, THE CHURCH ON THE WAY, VAN NUYS, CALIFORNIA

Dr. John Maxwell's latest work, *The 21 Irrefutable Laws of Leadership,* is a must-have success manual for all leaders who are committed to leading. It will be of immediate and immense help to anyone in a leadership position. This is his best. It's a treasure!

JACK AND GARRY KINDER
WELL-KNOWN AUTHORS, SPEAKERS, AND CONSULTANTS

John Maxwell understands what it takes to be a leader, and he puts it within reach in *The 21 Irrefutable Laws of Leadership.* I recommend this book to anyone who desires success at the highest level, whether on the ball field, in the boardroom, or from the pulpit.

TOM LANDRY
FORMER HEAD COACH, DALLAS COWBOYS

From his vast experience in the field of leadership, John Maxwell has delivered a truly valuable book, from which I believe every Christian man can benefit. In typical Maxwell style, filled with wisdom, wit, and passion, John provides a wealth of practical insights on what it takes to be a successful leader. I *highly* recommend this publication to every man who is striving to fulfill God's call to leadership, whether it be in his family, his church, his work, or in the wider community.

BILL McCARTNEY
FOUNDER & CEO, PROMISE KEEPERS

The laws of leadership are, indeed, irrefutable . . . and now they are comprehensively presented by the foremost expert on the subject. Either by instinct or by learning, you cannot be a successful leader in today's world without observing these laws. This book is a fast read, but it will change the rest of your life.

BARRY MEGUIAR
PRESIDENT/CEO, MEGUIAR'S, INC.

Maxwell's own experience, professionalism, and leadership effectiveness are reflected throughout the time-proven information on leadership presented in this book. Skillfully using real people and true stories, Maxwell brings to life *The 21 Irrefutable Laws of Leadership.* His well-written book will move leaders and would-be leaders out of their comfort zone to higher levels of leadership.

PAUL J. MEYER, FOUNDER,
SUCCESS MOTIVATION INSTITUTE, INC.
LEADERSHIP MANAGEMENT, INC.
MEYER FAMILY ENTERPRISES (40 COMPANIES)

Dr. Maxwell hits leadership for the millennium head-on. Every executive needs this in his or her library. Great job. Thanks.

BRUCE PARKER
PRUDENTIAL INSURANCE

This is the essential Maxwell book. His "21 Laws," hammered out of a lifetime of learning, will revolutionize your ability to make a difference. In no-nonsense, practical terms, John shows us how to turn big ideas into bold realities. He not only provides the motivation, but the know-how for moving mountains. Everyone needs this book.

LES PARROTT III, PH.D.
AUTHOR, *HIGH-MAINTENANCE RELATIONSHIPS*

An exciting summary of thirty years of experience by John Maxwell in leadership and leadership development! These laws, if obeyed, can be life changing! A holistic approach to the leadership phenomena! Ideas captured in a single book and presented in a way to challenge us personally to higher levels of personal effectiveness.

FRED ROACH
PRESIDENT, THE LEADERSHIP CENTER, BAYLOR HEALTH CARE SYSTEM

John Maxwell has been learning and successfully applying *The 21 Irrefutable Laws of Leadership* for thirty years. I am delighted that he has put them into this exciting, accessible book so that you can learn them and apply them too!

DR. ROBERT H. SCHULLER
FOUNDING PASTOR, CRYSTAL CATHEDRAL MINISTRIES

John Maxwell continues to help us build momentum in the cause of Christ. This is an insightful and strategic perspective on leadership. If you want to lead or are deep in the waters of leadership, this will be an important book for you.

DR. JOSEPH M. STOWELL
PRESIDENT, MOODY BIBLE INSTITUTE

John Maxwell is the leading authority on leadership in America today. *The 21 Irrefutable Laws of Leadership* is a powerful compilation of John's knowledge of leadership. This book has impacted my life deeply.

PAT WILLIAMS
SR. EXECUTIVE VICE PRESIDENT, ORLANDO MAGIC

The 21 Irrefutable Laws of Leadership is helpful and easy to read, yet profound in its depth and clarity. It's loaded with hope, direction, encouragement, and specific procedures. It's principle-based with precise, clear-cut directions to provide a willing student with the necessary tools to fulfill his or her leadership role.

ZIG ZIGLAR
AUTHOR AND MOTIVATIONAL TEACHER

*To the hundreds of thousands of people
to whom I've taught leadership over the years
through conferences and books . . .*

and

*To you—
the person wanting to become a better leader
because
everything rises and falls on leadership*

CONTENTS

1. THE LAW OF THE LID   1

*Leadership Ability Determines a
Person's Level of Effectiveness*

Brothers Dick and Maurice came as close as they could to living the American Dream—without making it. Instead a guy named Ray did it with the company they had founded. It happened because they didn't know the Law of the Lid.

2. THE LAW OF INFLUENCE   11

*The True Measure of Leadership Is Influence—
Nothing More, Nothing Less*

Her husband had everything: wealth, privilege, position, and a royal title. Yet instead of him, Princess Diana won over the whole world. Why? She understood the Law of Influence.

3. THE LAW OF PROCESS   21

Leadership Develops Daily, Not in a Day

Theodore Roosevelt helped create a world power, won a Nobel Peace Prize, and became president of the United States. But today you wouldn't even know his name if he hadn't known the Law of Process.

4. THE LAW OF NAVIGATION 33

Anyone Can Steer the Ship, But It Takes a Leader to Chart the Course

Using a fail-safe compass, Scott led his team of adventurers to the end of the earth—and to inglorious deaths. They would have lived if only he, their leader, had known the Law of Navigation.

5. THE LAW OF E. F. HUTTON 43

When the Real Leader Speaks, People Listen

Young John went into his first board meeting thinking he was in charge. He soon found out who the real leader was and learned the Law of E. F. Hutton in the process.

6. THE LAW OF SOLID GROUND 55

Trust Is the Foundation of Leadership

If only Robert McNamara had known the Law of Solid Ground, the War in Vietnam—and everything that happened at home because of it—might have turned out differently.

7. THE LAW OF RESPECT 67

People Naturally Follow Leaders Stronger Than Themselves

The odds were stacked against her in just about every possible way, but thousands and thousands of people called her their leader. Why? Because they could not escape the power of the Law of Respect.

8. THE LAW OF INTUITION 77

Leaders Evaluate Everything with a Leadership Bias

How is it that time after time Norman Schwarzkopf was able to sense problems while other leaders around him got blindsided? The answer lies in the factor that separates the great leaders from the merely good ones: the Law of Intuition.

9. THE LAW OF MAGNETISM   89

Who You Are Is Who You Attract

Why are the Dallas Cowboys, once revered as "America's Team," now so often reviled and the subject of controversy? The Law of Magnetism makes it clear.

10. THE LAW OF CONNECTION 99

Leaders Touch a Heart Before They Ask for a Hand

Elizabeth Dole has mastered it. If husband Bob had done the same, he might have become the forty-third president of the United States. It's called the Law of Connection.

11. THE LAW OF THE INNER CIRCLE   109

A Leader's Potential Is Determined by Those Closest to Him

John already used time management to the fullest, but he wanted to accomplish more. His priorities were already leveraged to the hilt, and there were no more minutes in a day! How did he go to a new level? He practiced the Law of the Inner Circle.

12. THE LAW OF EMPOWERMENT   121

Only Secure Leaders Give Power to Others

Henry Ford is considered an icon of American business for revolutionizing the automobile industry. So what caused him to stumble so badly that his son feared Ford Motor Company would go out of business? He was held captive by the Law of Empowerment.

13. THE LAW OF REPRODUCTION   133

It Takes a Leader to Raise Up a Leader

What do the top NFL head coaches have in common? You can trace their leadership ability to just a handful of mentors. That's also true for hundreds of CEOs. More than 80 percent of all leaders are the result of the Law of Reproduction.

14. THE LAW OF BUY-IN   143

People Buy Into the Leader, Then the Vision

The first time Judy Estrim started up a company, it took her six months to find the money. The second time it took her about six minutes. What made the difference? The Law of Buy-In.

15. THE LAW OF VICTORY   153

Leaders Find a Way for the Team to Win

What saved England from the Blitz, broke apartheid's back in South Africa, and won the Chicago Bulls multiple world championships? In all three cases the answer is the same. Their leaders lived by the Law of Victory.

16. THE LAW OF THE BIG MO   165

Momentum Is a Leader's Best Friend

Jaime Escalante has been called the best teacher in America. But his teaching ability is only half the story. His and Garfield High School's success came because of the Law of the Big Mo.

17. THE LAW OF PRIORITIES   175

Leaders Understand That Activity Is Not Necessarily Accomplishment

Jack Welch took a company that was already flying high and rocketed it into the stratosphere. What did he use as the launching pad? The Law of Priorities, of course.

18. THE LAW OF SACRIFICE   183

A Leader Must Give Up to Go Up

He was one of the nation's most vocal critics on government interference in business. So why did Lee Iacocca go before Congress with his hat in his hand for loan guarantees? He did it because he understood the Law of Sacrifice.

19. THE LAW OF TIMING   193

When to Lead Is As Important As What to Do and Where to Go

It got him elected president of the United States. It also cost him the presidency. What is it? Something that may stand between you and your ability to lead effectively. It's called the Law of Timing.

20. THE LAW OF EXPLOSIVE GROWTH   205

To Add Growth, Lead Followers—To Multiply, Lead Leaders

How did a man in a developing country take his organization from 700 people to more than 14,000 in only seven years? He did it using leader's math. That's the secret of the Law of Explosive Growth.

21. THE LAW OF LEGACY 215

A Leader's Lasting Value Is Measured by Succession

When many companies lose their CEO, they go into a tailspin. But when Roberto Goizueta died, Coca-Cola didn't even hiccup. Why? Before his death, Goizueta lived by the Law of Legacy.

FOREWORD

Y OU ARE GOING TO LOVE this book—whether it is the first leadership book in your collection or the fiftieth—because you can immediately apply the life-changing principles and procedures in your personal, family, and business life. There is no "ivory tower" theory in this book. Instead, it is loaded with unchanging leadership principles confirmed by the real-world experiences of John Maxwell and the many people he writes about.

The 21 Irrefutable Laws of Leadership is a powerful, definitive statement of the timeless laws you simply *must* follow if you want to be a great leader—at home, on the job, in church, or wherever you are called on to lead.

In each chapter, John goes straight to the heart of a profound leadership law, showing you through the successes and failures of others how you can apply the law in your life. And you *can* apply each of the laws. If you're a willing student, you can learn the 21 laws and put them into practice.

What a priceless treasure leadership authority John Maxwell offers as he boils everything he's learned about leadership down into such usable form! Once you apply these leadership laws, you'll notice leaders all around you putting into action (or breaking) the Law of E. F. Hutton, the Law of the Big Mo, and the rest.

I heartily recommend *The 21 Irrefutable Laws of Leadership*. It is helpful and easy to read, yet profound in its depth and clarity. It's loaded with hope, direction, encouragement, and specific procedures. It's principle-based with precise, clear-cut directions to provide you with the necessary tools to fulfill your leadership role.

If you are new to leadership, this book will jump-start your leadership career. If you are an experienced leader with blue-chip credentials, this book will make you an even better leader. It's good—very good.

Zig Ziglar

ACKNOWLEDGMENTS

I'D LIKE TO THANK the many leaders who helped me while I was working on this book. From INJOY: Dick Peterson, Dave Sutherland, Dan Reiland, Tim Elmore, and Dennis Worden. From Thomas Nelson: Rolf Zettersten, Ron Land, Mike Hyatt, Victor Oliver, and Rob Birkhead.

I must say thank you to Brian Hampton, my managing editor at Nelson, for his patience and assistance as we worked through the manuscript.

I also want to thank my assistant, Linda Eggers, whose great heart and incredible service make me a better leader.

Finally, I want to thank Charlie Wetzel, my writer, and his wife, Stephanie. This book would not have been written without their help.

INTRODUCTION

I HAVE THE PRIVILEGE of teaching leadership across the country and around the globe, and I often get the opportunity to talk with people who are attending one of my conferences for a second, third, or even fourth time. At a recent conference here in the United States, a man in his late fifties whom I had met several years before came up and spoke to me during a break. He grabbed my hand and shook it vigorously. "Learning leadership has changed my life," he said. "But I sure wish I had heard you twenty years ago."

"No, you don't," I answered with a chuckle.

"What do you mean?" he said. "I would have achieved so much more! If I had known these leadership principles twenty years ago, I'd be in a totally different place in life. Your leadership laws have fueled my vision. They've given me the desire to learn more about leadership and accomplish my goals. If I'd learned this twenty years ago, I could have done some things that I had never even dreamed possible."

"Maybe you would have," I answered. "But twenty years ago, I wouldn't have been able to teach them to you. It has taken me my entire lifetime to learn and apply the laws of leadership to my life."

As I write this, I am fifty-one years old. I've spent more than thirty years in professional leadership positions. I've founded four companies. And I focus my time and energy on doing what makes a positive impact in the lives of people. But I've also made a lot of mistakes along the way—more than most people I know. Every success and every failure has been an invaluable lesson in what it means to lead.

As I travel and speak to organizations and individuals, people frequently ask me to define the essentials of leadership. "If you were to take everything you've learned about leadership over the years and boil it down into a short list," they ask, "what would it be?"

This book is my answer to that often-asked question. It has taken me a lifetime to learn these 21 Irrefutable Laws of Leadership. My desire is to communicate them to you as simply and clearly as possible. And it sure won't hurt if we have some fun along the way.

One of the most important truths I've learned over the years is this: Leadership is leadership, no matter where you go or what you do. Times change. Technology marches forward. Cultures vary from place to place. But the true principles of leadership are constant—whether you're looking at the citizens of ancient Greece, the Hebrews in the Old Testament, the armies of the last two hundred years, the rulers of modern Europe, the pastors in local churches, or the businesspeople of today's global economy. Leadership principles stand the test of time. They are irrefutable.

As you read the following chapters, I'd like you to keep in mind four ideas:

1. **The laws can be learned.** Some are easier to understand and apply than others, but every one of them can be acquired.

2. **The laws can stand alone.** Each law complements all the others, but you don't need one in order to learn another.

3. **The laws carry consequences with them.** Apply the laws, and people will follow you. Violate or ignore them, and you will not be able to lead others.

4. **These laws are the foundation of leadership.** Once you learn the principles, you have to practice them and apply them to your life.

Whether you are a follower who is just beginning to discover the impact of leadership or a natural leader who already has followers, you can become a better leader. As you read about the laws, you'll recognize that you may already practice some of them effectively. Other laws will expose weaknesses you didn't know you had. But the greater the number of laws you learn, the better leader you will become. Each law is like a tool, ready to be picked up and used to help you achieve your dreams and add value to other people. Pick up even one, and you will become a better leader. Learn them all, and people will gladly follow you.

Now, let's open the toolbox together.

THE LAW OF THE LID

*Leadership Ability Determines
a Person's Level of Effectiveness*

I OFTEN OPEN MY LEADERSHIP conferences by explaining the Law of the Lid because it helps people understand the value of leadership. If you can get a handle on this law, you will see the incredible impact of leadership on every aspect of life. So here it is: Leadership ability is the lid that determines a person's level of effectiveness. The lower an individual's ability to lead, the lower the lid on his potential. The higher the leadership, the greater the effectiveness. To give you an example, if your leadership rates an 8, then your effectiveness can never be greater than a 7. If your leadership is only a 4, then your effectiveness will be no higher than a 3. Your leadership ability—for better or for worse—always determines your effectiveness and the potential impact of your organization.

Let me tell you a story that illustrates the Law of the Lid. In 1930, two young brothers named Dick and Maurice moved from New Hampshire to California in search of the American Dream. They had just gotten out of high school, and they saw few opportunities back home. So they headed straight for Hollywood where they eventually found jobs on a movie studio set.

After a while, their entrepreneurial spirit and interest in the entertainment industry prompted them to open a theater in Glendale, a town about five miles northeast of Hollywood. But despite all their efforts, the brothers just couldn't make the business profitable. In the four years they ran the theater, they weren't able to consistently generate enough money to pay the one hundred dollars a month rent that their landlord required.

A NEW OPPORTUNITY

The brothers' desire for success was strong, so they kept looking for better business opportunities. In 1937, they finally struck on something that worked. They opened a small drive-in restaurant in Pasadena, located just east of Glendale. People in southern California had become very dependent on their cars, and the culture was changing to accommodate that, including its businesses.

Drive-in restaurants were a phenomenon that sprang up in the early thirties, and they were becoming very popular. Rather than being invited into a dining room to eat, customers would drive into a parking lot around a small restaurant, place their orders with carhops, and receive their food on trays right in their cars. The food was served on china plates complete with glassware and metal utensils. It was a timely idea in a society that was becoming faster paced and increasingly mobile.

Dick and Maurice's tiny drive-in restaurant was a great success, and in 1940, they decided to move the operation to San Bernardino, a working-class boomtown fifty miles east of Los Angeles. They built a larger facility and expanded their menu from hot dogs, fries, and shakes to include barbecued beef and pork sandwiches, hamburgers, and other items. Their business exploded. Annual sales reached

$200,000, and the brothers found themselves splitting $50,000 in profits every year—a sum that put them in the town's financial elite.

In 1948, their intuition told them that times were changing, and they made modifications to their restaurant business. They eliminated the carhops and started serving only walk-up customers. And they also streamlined everything. They reduced their menu and focused on selling hamburgers. They eliminated plates, glassware, and metal utensils, switching to paper products instead. They reduced their costs and the prices they charged customers. They also created what they called the Speedy Service System. Their kitchen became like an assembly line, where each person focused on service with speed. Their goal was to fill each customer's order in thirty seconds or less. And they succeeded. By the mid-1950s, annual revenue hit $350,000, and by then, Dick and Maurice split net profits of about $100,000 each year.

Who were these brothers? Back in those days, you could have found out by driving to their small restaurant on the corner of Fourteenth and E Streets in San Bernardino. On the front of the small octagonal building hung a neon sign that said simply MCDONALD'S HAMBURGERS. Dick and Maurice McDonald had hit the great American jackpot, and the rest, as they say, is history, right? Wrong. The McDonalds never went any farther because their weak leadership put a lid on their ability to succeed.

THE STORY BEHIND THE STORY

It's true that the McDonald brothers were financially secure. Theirs was one of the most profitable restaurant enterprises in the country, and they felt that they had a hard time spending all the money they made. Their genius was in customer service and kitchen organization. That talent led to the creation of a new system of food and beverage service. In fact, their talent was so widely known in food service circles that people started writing them and visiting from all over the country to learn more about their methods. At one point, they received as many as three hundred calls and letters every month.

That led them to the idea of marketing the McDonald's concept. The idea of franchising restaurants wasn't new. It had been around for several decades. To the McDonald brothers, it looked like a way to make money without having to open another restaurant themselves. In 1952, they got started, but their effort was a dismal failure. The reason was simple. They lacked the leadership necessary to make it effective. Dick and Maurice were good restaurant owners. They understood how to run a business, make their systems efficient, cut costs, and increase profits. They were efficient managers. But they were not leaders. Their thinking patterns clamped a lid down on what they could do and become. At the height of their success, Dick and Maurice found themselves smack-dab against the Law of the Lid.

THE BROTHERS PARTNER WITH A LEADER

In 1954, the brothers hooked up with a man named Ray Kroc who *was* a leader. Kroc had been running a small company he founded, which sold machines for making milk shakes. He knew about McDonald's. Their restaurant was one of his best customers. And as soon as he visited the store, he had a vision for its potential. In his mind he could see the restaurant going nationwide in hundreds of markets. He soon struck a deal with Dick and Maurice, and in 1955, he formed McDonald's System, Inc. (later called the McDonald's Corporation).

Kroc immediately bought the rights to a franchise so that he could use it as a model and prototype to sell other franchises. Then he began to assemble a team and build an organization to make McDonald's a nationwide entity. He recruited and hired the sharpest people he could find, and as his team grew in size and ability, his people developed additional recruits with leadership skill.

In the early years, Kroc sacrificed a lot. Though he was in his midfifties, he worked long hours just as he had when he first got started in business thirty years earlier. He eliminated many frills at home, including his country club membership, which he later said added ten strokes to his golf game. During his first eight years with McDonald's, he took no salary. Not only that, but he personally borrowed money from the bank and against his life insurance to help cover the salaries of a few key leaders he wanted on the team. His sacrifice and his leadership paid off. In 1961 for the sum of $2.7 million, Kroc bought the exclusive rights to McDonald's from the brothers, and he proceeded to turn it into an American institution and global entity. The "lid" in the life and leadership of Ray Kroc was obviously much higher than that of his predecessors.

In the years that Dick and Maurice McDonald had attempted to franchise their food service system, they managed to sell the concept to just fifteen buyers, only ten of whom actually opened restaurants. And even in that small enterprise, their limited leadership and vision were hindrances. For example, when their first franchisee, Neil Fox of Phoenix, told the brothers that he wanted to call his restaurant McDonald's, Dick's response was, "What . . . for? McDonald's means nothing in Phoenix."

On the other hand, the leadership lid in Ray Kroc's life was sky high. Between 1955 and 1959, Kroc succeeded in opening 100 restaurants. Four years after that, there were 500 McDonald's. Today the company has opened more than 21,000 restaurants in no fewer than 100 countries.[1] Leadership ability—or more specifically the lack of leadership ability—was the lid on the McDonald brothers' effectiveness.

SUCCESS WITHOUT LEADERSHIP

I believe that success is within the reach of just about everyone. But I also believe that personal success without leadership ability brings only

> *The higher you want to climb, the more you need leadership. The greater the impact you want to make, the greater your influence needs to be.*

limited effectiveness. A person's impact is only a fraction of what it could be with good leadership. The higher you want to climb, the more you need leadership. The greater the impact you want to make, the greater your influence needs to be. Whatever you will accomplish is restricted by your ability to lead others.

Let me give you a picture of what I mean. Let's say that when it comes to success, you're an 8 (on a scale from 1 to 10). That's pretty good. I think it would be safe to say that the McDonald brothers were in that range. But let's also say that your leadership ability is only a 1. Your level of effectiveness would look like this:

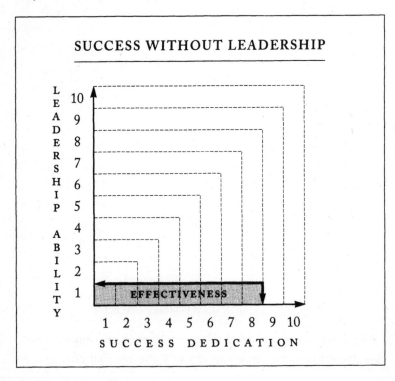

SUCCESS WITHOUT LEADERSHIP

LEADERSHIP ABILITY

EFFECTIVENESS

1 2 3 4 5 6 7 8 9 10

SUCCESS DEDICATION

To increase your level of effectiveness, you have a couple of choices. You could work very hard to increase your dedication to success and excellence—to work toward becoming a 10. It's possible that you could make it to that level, though the Law of Diminishing Returns says that the effort it would take to increase those last two points might take more energy than it did to achieve the first eight. If you really killed yourself, you might increase your success by that 25 percent.

But you have another option. Let's say that instead you work hard to increase your level of *leadership*. Over the course of time, you develop yourself as a leader, and eventually, your leadership ability becomes, say, a 6. Visually, the results would look like this:

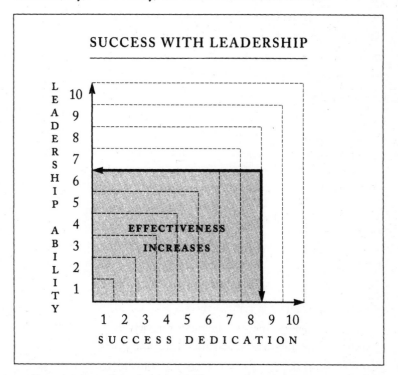

SUCCESS WITH LEADERSHIP

LEADERSHIP ABILITY

EFFECTIVENESS INCREASES

SUCCESS DEDICATION

By raising your leadership ability—without increasing your success dedication at all—you can increase your original effectiveness by 500 percent! If you were to raise your leadership to 8, where it matched your success dedication, you would increase your effectiveness by 700 percent! Leadership has a multiplying effect. I've seen its impact over and over again in all kinds of businesses and non-profit organizations. And that's why I've taught leadership for more than twenty years.

TO CHANGE THE DIRECTION OF THE ORGANIZATION, CHANGE THE LEADER

Leadership ability is always the lid on personal and organizational effectiveness. If the leadership is strong, the lid is high. But if it's not, then the organization is limited. That's why in times of trouble, organizations naturally look for new leadership. When the country is experiencing hard times, it elects a new president. When a company

> *Personal and organizational effectiveness is proportionate to the strength of leadership.*

is losing money, it hires a new CEO. When a church is floundering, it searches for a new senior pastor. When a sports team keeps losing, it looks for a new head coach.

The relationship between leadership and effectiveness is evident in sports. For example, if you look at professional sports organizations, the talent on the team is rarely the issue. Just about every team has highly talented players. The leadership provided by the coach—and several key players—makes the difference. To change the effectiveness of the team, lift up the leadership of the coach. That's the Law of the Lid.

A sports team with a long history of leadership and effectiveness is Notre Dame. The school's football teams have won more national championships than any other team in the country. Over the years, the Fighting Irish have won more than three-fourths of all their games (an incredible .759 winning percentage). In fact, two of their former head coaches, Knute Rockne and Frank Leahy, have the highest winning percentages in NCAA history.

Back in the early 1980s, Notre Dame hired Gerry Faust as its head football coach. He was following two great coaches: Ara Parseghian and Dan Devine, both of whom had won national championships during their tenure and both of whom were eventually inducted into the National Football Foundation Hall of Fame. Prior to coming to Notre Dame, Faust had compiled an incredible record of 174-17-2 during his eighteen years as the head coach at Moeller High School. His teams experienced seven undefeated seasons and won six Ohio state titles. Four teams he coached were considered the best in the nation.

But when he arrived at Notre Dame, it didn't take long for people to discover that he was in over his head. As a coach and strategist, he was effective, but he didn't have the leadership ability necessary to make it at the college level. During his five seasons at the university, he compiled a 30-26-1 record and winning percentage of .535, third worst in Notre Dame's one-hundred-plus-year history of college football. Faust coached only one other college team after that, the University of Akron, where he finished with an overall losing record of 43-53-3. He was another casualty of the Law of the Lid.

Wherever you look, you can find smart, talented, successful people who are able to go only so far because of the limitations of their leadership. For example, when Apple got started in the late 1970s, Steve Wozniak was the brains behind the Apple computer. His leadership lid was low, but that was not the case for his partner, Steve Jobs. His lid was so high that he built a world-class organization and gave it a nine-digit value. That's the impact of the Law of the Lid.

A few years ago, I met Don Stephenson, the chairman of Global Hospitality Resources, Inc., of San Diego, California, an international hospitality advisory and consulting firm. Over lunch, I asked him about his organization. Today he primarily does consulting, but back then his company took over the management of hotels and resorts that weren't doing well financially. They oversaw many excellent facilities such as La Costa in southern California.

> *You can find smart, talented, successful people who are able to go only so far because of the limitations of their leadership.*

Don said that whenever they came into an organization to take it over, they always started by doing two things: First, they trained all the staff to improve their level of service to the customers; and second, they fired the leader. When he told me that, I was at first surprised.

"You *always* fire him?" I asked. "Every time?"

"That's right. Every time," he said.

"Don't you talk to the person first—to check him out to see if he's a good leader?" I said.

"No," he answered. "If he'd been a good leader, the organization wouldn't be in the mess it's in."

And I thought to myself, *Of course. It's the Law of the Lid.* To reach the highest level of effectiveness, you have to raise the lid—one way or another.

The good news is that getting rid of the leader isn't the *only* way. Just as I teach in conferences that there is a lid, I also teach that you can raise it—but that's the subject of another law of leadership.

2

THE LAW OF INFLUENCE

The True Measure of Leadership Is
Influence—Nothing More, Nothing Less

I F YOU DON'T HAVE INFLUENCE, you will *never* be able to lead others. So how do you measure influence? Here's a story to answer that question. In late summer of 1997, people were jolted by two events that occurred less than a week apart: the deaths of Princess Diana and Mother Teresa. On the surface, the two women could not have been more different. One was a tall, young, glamorous princess from England who circulated in the highest society. The other, a Nobel Peace Prize recipient, was a small, elderly Catholic nun born in Albania, who served the poorest of the poor in Calcutta, India.

What's incredible is that their impact was remarkably similar. In a 1996 poll published by the London *Daily Mail,* Princess Diana and Mother Teresa were voted in first and second places as the world's two most caring people. That's something that doesn't happen unless you have a lot of influence. How did someone like Diana come to be regarded in the same way as Mother Teresa? The answer is that she demonstrated the power of the Law of Influence.

DIANA CAPTURED
THE WORLD'S IMAGINATION

In 1981, Diana became the most talked-about person on the globe when she married Prince Charles of England. Nearly 1 billion people watched Diana's wedding ceremony televised from St. Paul's Cathedral. And since that day, it seemed people never could get enough news about her. People were intrigued with Diana, a commoner who had once been a kindergarten teacher. At first she seemed painfully shy and totally overwhelmed by all the attention she and her new husband were receiving. Early in their marriage, some reports stated that Diana wasn't very happy performing the duties expected of her as a royal princess. However, in time she adjusted to her new role. As she started traveling and representing the royal family around the world at various functions, she quickly made it her goal to serve others and raise funds for numerous charitable causes. And during the process, she built many important relationships—with politicians, organizers of humanitarian causes, entertainers, and heads of state. At first, she was simply a spokesperson and catalyst for fund-raising, but as time went by, her influence increased—and so did her ability to make things happen.

Diana started rallying people to causes such as AIDS research, care for people with leprosy, and a ban on land mines. She was quite influential in bringing that last issue to the attention of the world's leaders. On a visit to the United States just months before her death, she met with members of the Clinton administration to convince them to support the Oslo conference banning the devices. And a few weeks later, they made changes in their position. Patrick Fuller of the British Red Cross said, "The attention she drew to the issue influenced Clinton. She put the issue on the world agenda, there's no doubt about that."[1]

THE EMERGENCE OF A LEADER

In the beginning, Diana's title had merely given her a platform to address others, but she soon became a person of influence in her own right. In 1996 when she was divorced from Prince Charles, she lost her title, but that loss didn't at all diminish her impact on others. Instead, her influence continued to increase while that of her former husband and in-laws declined—despite their royal titles and position. Why? Diana instinctively understood the Law of Influence.

> *"You have achieved excellence as a leader when people will follow you everywhere if only out of curiosity."*
> —Colin Powell

Ironically, even in death Diana continued to influence others. When her funeral was broadcast on television and BBC Radio, it was translated into forty-four languages. NBC estimated that the total audience numbered as many as 2.5 billion people—more than twice the number of people who watched her wedding.

THE QUESTION OF LEADERSHIP

Princess Diana has been characterized in many ways. But one word that I've never heard used to describe her is *leader*. Yet that's what she was. Ultimately, she made things happen because she was an influencer, and leadership is influence—nothing more, nothing less.

LEADERSHIP IS NOT . . .

People have so many misconceptions about leadership. When they hear that someone has an impressive title or an assigned leadership position, they assume that he is a leader. *Sometimes* that's true. But titles don't have much value when it comes to leading. True leadership cannot be awarded, appointed, or assigned. It comes only from influence, and that can't be mandated. It must be earned. The only thing a title can buy is a little time—either to increase your level of influence with others or to erase it.

FIVE MYTHS ABOUT LEADERSHIP

There are plenty of misconceptions and myths that people embrace about leaders and leadership. Here are five common ones:

1. THE MANAGEMENT MYTH

A widespread misunderstanding is that leading and managing are one and the same. Up until a few years ago, books that claimed to be on leadership were often really about management. The main difference between the two is that leadership is about influencing people to follow, while management focuses on maintaining systems and processes. As former Chrysler chairman and CEO Lee Iacocca wryly commented, "Sometimes even the best manager is like the little boy with the big dog, waiting to see where the dog wants to go so that he can take him there."

> *The only thing a title can buy is a little time—either to increase your level of influence with others or to erase it.*

The best way to test whether a person can lead rather than just manage is to ask him to create positive change. Managers can maintain direction, but they can't change it. To move people in a new direction, you need influence.

2. THE ENTREPRENEUR MYTH

Frequently, people assume that all salespeople and entrepreneurs are leaders. But that's not always the case. You may remember the

Ronco commercials that appeared on television years ago. They sold items such as the Veg-O-Matic, Pocket Fisherman, and Inside-the-Shell Egg Scrambler. Those products were the brainchildren of an entrepreneur named Ron Popeil. Called the salesman of the century, he has also appeared in numerous infomercials for products such as spray-on relief for baldness and food dehydrating devices.

Popeil is certainly enterprising, innovative, and successful, especially if you measure him by the $300 million in sales his products have earned. But that doesn't make him a leader. People may be buying what he has to sell, but they're not following him. At best, he is able to persuade people for a moment, but he holds no long-term influence with them.

3. THE KNOWLEDGE MYTH

Sir Francis Bacon said, "Knowledge is power." Most people, believing power is the essence of leadership, naturally assume that those who possess knowledge and intelligence are leaders. But that isn't automatically true. You can visit any major university and meet brilliant research scientists and philosophers whose ability to think is so high that it's off the charts, but whose ability to lead is so low that it doesn't even register on the charts. IQ doesn't necessarily equate to leadership.

4. THE PIONEER MYTH

Another misconception is that anyone who is out in front of the crowd is a leader. But being first isn't always the same as leading. For example, Sir Edmund Hillary was the first man to reach the summit of Mount Everest. Since his historic ascent in 1953, many people have "followed" him in achieving that feat. But that doesn't make Hillary a leader. He wasn't even the leader on that particular expedition. John Hunt was. And when Hillary traveled to the South Pole in 1958 as part of the Commonwealth Trans-Antarctic Expedition, he was accompanying another leader, Sir Vivian Fuchs. To be a leader, a person has to not only be out front, but also have people intentionally coming behind him, following his lead, and acting on his vision.

5. THE POSITION MYTH

As mentioned earlier, the greatest misunderstanding about leadership is that people think it is based on position, but it's not. Stanley Huffty affirmed, "It's not the position that makes the leader; it's the leader that makes the position."

Look at what happened several years ago at Cordiant, the advertising agency formerly known as Saatchi & Saatchi. In 1994, institutional investors at Saatchi & Saatchi forced the board of directors to dismiss Maurice Saatchi, the company's CEO. What was the result? Several executives followed him out. So did many of the company's largest accounts, including British Airways and Mars, the candy maker. Saatchi's influence was so great that his departure caused the company's stock to fall immediately from $8⅝ to $4 per share.[2] What happened is a result of the Law of Influence. Saatchi lost his title and position, but he continued to be the leader.

> "It's not the position that makes the leader; it's the leader that makes the position."
> —Stanley Huffty

WHO'S THE REAL LEADER?

I personally learned the Law of Influence when I accepted my first job out of college at a small church in rural Indiana. I went in with all the right credentials. I was hired as the senior pastor, which meant that I possessed the position and title of leader in that organization. I had the proper college degree. I had even been ordained. In addition, I had been trained by my father who was an excellent pastor and a very high-profile leader in the denomination. It made for a good-looking résumé—but it didn't make me a leader. At my first board meeting, I quickly found out who was the real leader of that church. (I'll tell you the whole story in the Law of E. F. Hutton.) By the time I took my next position three years later, I had learned the Law of Influence. I recognized that hard work was required to gain influence in any organization and to earn the right to become the leader.

LEADERSHIP IS . . .

Leadership is influence—nothing more, nothing less. When you become a student of leaders, as I am, you recognize people's level of influence in everyday situations all around you. Let me give you an example. In 1997, I moved to Atlanta, Georgia. In that same year, Dan Reeves became the coach of the NFL's Atlanta Falcons. I was glad to hear that. Reeves is an excellent coach and leader. Though he had most recently coached the New York Giants, Reeves made his reputation as the head coach of the Denver Broncos. From 1981 to 1992, he compiled an excellent 117-79-1 record, earned three Super Bowl appearances, and received NFL Coach of the Year honors three times.

Despite Reeves's success in Denver, he didn't always experience smooth sailing. He was known to have had disagreements with quarterback John Elway and assistant coach Mike Shanahan. What was the reason for the problem? It was said that during the 1989 season, Shanahan and Elway sometimes worked on their own offensive game plan, ignoring Reeves's wishes. I don't know if that was true, but if it was, then Shanahan, not Reeves, had developed greater influence with the Denver quarterback. It didn't matter that Reeves held the title and position of head coach. It didn't even matter how good a coach Reeves was. Shanahan had become the more influential leader in the quarterback's life. And leadership is influence.

Shanahan left the Broncos at the end of that season, but he returned in 1995 as the team's head coach. He became in title what he evidently already had been in terms of influence to some of the players: their leader. And that leadership has now paid off. In January of 1998, he led the Denver Broncos franchise and quarterback John Elway to their first Super Bowl victory.

LEADERSHIP WITHOUT LEVERAGE

I admire and respect the leadership of my good friend Bill Hybels, the senior pastor of Willow Creek Community Church in South Barrington, Illinois, the largest church in North America. Bill says he believes that the church is the most leadership-intensive enterprise in society. A lot of businesspeople I know are surprised when they hear that statement, but I think Bill is right. What is the basis of his belief? Positional leadership doesn't work in volunteer organizations. Because a leader doesn't have leverage—or influence—he is ineffective. In other organizations, the person who has position has incredible leverage. In the military, leaders can use rank and, if all else fails, throw people into the brig. In business, bosses have tremendous leverage in the form of salary, benefits, and perks. Most followers are pretty cooperative when their livelihood is at stake.

> "The very essence of all power to influence lies in getting the other person to participate."
> —Harry A. Overstreet

But in voluntary organizations, such as churches, the only thing that works is leadership in its purest form. Leaders have only their influence to aid them. And as Harry A. Overstreet observed, "The very essence of all power to influence lies in getting the other person to participate." Followers in voluntary organizations cannot be forced to get on board. If the leader has no influence with them, then they won't follow. When I recently shared that observation with a group of about

150 CEOs from the automobile industry, I saw lightbulbs going on all over the room. And when I gave them a piece of advice, they really got excited. I'm going to share that same advice with you: If you are a businessperson and you really want to find out whether your people are capable of leading, send them out to volunteer their time in the community. If they can get people to follow them while they're serving at the Red Cross, a United Way shelter, or their local church, then you know that they really do have influence—and leadership ability.

FROM COMMANDER TO PRIVATE
TO COMMANDER IN CHIEF

One of my favorite stories that illustrates the Law of Influence concerns Abraham Lincoln. In 1832, years before he became president, young Lincoln gathered together a group of men to fight in the Black Hawk War. In those days, the person who put together a volunteer company for the militia often became its leader and assumed a commanding rank. In this instance, Lincoln had the rank of captain.

But Lincoln had a problem. He knew nothing about soldiering. He had no prior military experience, and he knew nothing about tactics. He had trouble remembering the simplest military procedures. For example, one day Lincoln was marching a couple of dozen men across a field and needed to guide

> *By the end of his military service, Abraham Lincoln found his rightful place, having achieved the rank of private.*

them through a gate into another field. But he couldn't manage it. Recounting the incident later, Lincoln said, "I could not for the life of me remember the proper word of command for getting my company endwise. Finally, as we came near [the gate] I shouted: 'This company is dismissed for two minutes, when it will fall in again on the other side of the gate.'"[3]

As time went by, Lincoln's level of influence with others in the militia actually *decreased.* While other officers proved themselves and gained rank, Lincoln found himself going in the other direction. He began with the *title and position* of captain, but that did him little good. He couldn't overcome the Law of Influence. By the end of his military service, Abraham Lincoln found his rightful place, having achieved the rank of private.

Fortunately for Lincoln—and for the fate of our country—he overcame his inability to influence others. He followed his time in the military with undistinguished stints in the Illinois state legislature and the U.S. House of Representatives. But over time and with much effort and personal experience, he became a person of remarkable influence and impact.

Here is my favorite leadership proverb: "He who thinks he leads, but has no followers, is only taking a walk." If you can't influence others, they won't follow you. And if they won't follow, you're not a leader. That's the Law of Influence. No matter what anybody else tells you, remember that leadership is influence—nothing more, nothing less.

3

THE LAW OF PROCESS

Leadership Develops Daily, Not in a Day

A<small>NNE SCHEIBER WAS</small> 101 years old when she died in January of 1995. For years she had lived in a tiny, run-down, rent-controlled studio apartment in Manhattan. The paint on the walls was peeling, and the old bookcases that lined the walls were covered in dust. Rent was four hundred dollars a month.

Scheiber lived on Social Security and a small monthly pension, which she started receiving in 1943 when she retired as an auditor for the Internal Revenue Service. She hadn't done very well at the IRS. More specifically, the agency hadn't done right by her. Despite having a law degree and doing excellent work, she was never promoted. And when she retired at age fifty-one, she was making only $3,150 a year.

"She was treated very, very shabbily," said Benjamin Clark, who knew her as well as anyone did. "She really had to fend for herself in every way. It was really quite a struggle."

Scheiber was the model of thrift. She didn't spend money on herself. She didn't buy new furniture as the old pieces she owned became worn out. She didn't even subscribe to a newspaper. About once a week, she used to go to the public library to read the *Wall Street Journal.*

WINDFALL!

Imagine the surprise of Norman Lamm, the president of Yeshiva University in New York City, when he found out that Anne Scheiber, a little old lady whom he had never heard of—and who had never attended Yeshiva—left nearly her entire estate to the university.

"When I saw the will, it was mind blowing, such an unexpected windfall," said Lamm. "This woman has become a legend overnight."

The estate Anne Scheiber left to Yeshiva University was worth $22 million![1]

How in the world did a spinster who had been retired for fifty years build an eight-figure fortune?

Here's the answer. By the time she retired from the IRS in 1943, Anne Scheiber had managed to save $5,000. She invested that money in stocks. By 1950, she had made enough profit to buy 1,000 shares of Schering-Plough Corporation stock, then valued at $10,000. And she held on to that stock, letting its value build. Today, those original shares have split enough times to produce 128,000 shares, worth $7.5 million.[2]

The secret to Scheiber's success was that she spent most of her life building her worth. Whether her stock's values went up or down, she never sold it off with the thought, *I'm finished building; now it's time to cash out.* She was in for the long haul, the *really* long haul. When she earned dividends—which kept getting larger and larger—she reinvested them. She spent her whole lifetime building. While other older people worry that they may run out of funds before the end of their lives, the longer she lived, the wealthier she became. When it came to finances, Scheiber understood and applied the Law of Process.

LEADERSHIP IS LIKE INVESTING—IT COMPOUNDS

Becoming a leader is a lot like investing successfully in the stock market. If your hope is to make a fortune in a day, you're not going to be successful. What matters most is what you do day by day over the long haul. My friend Tag Short maintains, "The secret of our success is found in our daily agenda." If you continually invest in your leadership development, letting your "assets" compound, the inevitable result is growth over time.

> *Becoming a leader is a lot like investing successfully in the stock market. If your hope is to make a fortune in a day, you're not going to be successful.*

When I teach leadership at conferences, people inevitably ask me whether leaders are born. I always answer, "Yes, of course they are . . . I've yet to meet one that came into the world any other way!" We all laugh, and then I answer the real question—whether leadership is something a person either possesses or doesn't.

Although it's true that some people are born with greater natural gifts than others, the ability to lead is really a collection of skills, nearly all of which can be learned and improved. But that process doesn't happen overnight. Leadership is complicated. It has many facets: respect, experience, emotional strength, people skills, discipline, vision, momentum, timing—the list goes on. As you can see, many factors that come into play in leadership are intangible. That's why leaders require so much seasoning to be effective. That's why only now, at age fifty-one, do I feel that I am truly beginning to understand the many aspects of leadership with clarity.

LEADERS ARE LEARNERS

In a study of ninety top leaders from a variety of fields, leadership experts Warren Bennis and Burt Nanus made a discovery about the relationship between growth and leadership: "It is the capacity to develop and improve their skills that distinguishes leaders from their followers." Successful leaders are learners. And the learning process is ongoing, a result of self-discipline and perseverance. The goal each day must be to get a little better, to build on the previous day's progress.

THE FOUR PHASES OF LEADERSHIP GROWTH

Whether you do or don't have great natural ability for leadership, your development and progress will probably occur according to the following four phases:

PHASE 1—I DON'T KNOW WHAT I DON'T KNOW

Most people fail to recognize the value of leadership. They believe that leadership is only for a few—for the people at the top of the corporate ladder. They have no idea of the opportunities they're passing up when they don't learn to lead. This point was driven home for me when a college president shared with me that only a handful of students signed up for a leadership course offered by the school. Why? Only a few thought of themselves as leaders. If they had known that leadership is influence, and that in the course of each day most individuals usually try to influence at least four other people, their desire might have been sparked to learn more about the subject. It's unfortunate because as long as a person doesn't know what he doesn't know, he doesn't grow.

> *As long as a person doesn't know what he doesn't know, he doesn't grow.*

PHASE 2—I KNOW WHAT I DON'T KNOW

Usually at some point in life, we are placed in a leadership position only to look around and discover that no one is following us.

That's when we realize that we need to *learn* how to lead. And of course, that's when it's possible for the process to start. English Prime Minister Benjamin Disraeli wisely commented, "To be conscious that you are ignorant of the facts is a great step to knowledge."

That's what happened to me when I took my first leadership position in 1969. I had captained sports teams all my life and had been the student government president in college, so I already thought I was a leader. But when I tried to lead people in the real world, I found out the awful truth. That prompted me to start gathering resources and learning from them. I also had another idea: I wrote to the top ten leaders in my field and offered them one hundred dollars for a half hour of their time so that I could ask them questions. (That was quite a sum for me in 1969.) For the next several years, my wife, Margaret, and I planned every vacation around where those people lived. If a great leader in Cleveland said yes to my request, then that year we vacationed in Cleveland so that I could meet him. And my idea really paid off. Those men shared insights with me that I could have learned no other way.

> *"To be conscious that you are ignorant of the facts is a great step to knowledge."*
> —*Benjamin Disraeli*

PHASE 3—I GROW AND KNOW AND IT STARTS TO SHOW

When you recognize your lack of skill and begin the daily discipline of personal growth in leadership, exciting things start to happen.

A while back I was teaching a group of people in Denver, and in the crowd I noticed a really sharp nineteen-year-old named Brian. For a couple of days, I watched as he eagerly took notes. I talked to him a few times during breaks. When I got to the part of the seminar where I teach the Law of Process, I asked Brian to stand up so that I could talk while everyone listened. I said, "Brian, I've been watching you here, and I'm very impressed with how hungry you are to learn and glean and grow. I want to tell you a secret that will change your life." Everyone in the whole auditorium seemed to lean forward.

"I believe that in about twenty years, you can be a *great* leader. I want to encourage you to make yourself a lifelong learner of leadership. Read books, listen to tapes regularly, and keep attending seminars. And whenever you come across a golden nugget of truth or a significant quote, file it away for the future.

"It's not going to be easy," I said. "But in five years, you'll see progress as your influence becomes greater. In ten years you'll develop a competence that makes your leadership highly effective. And in twenty years, when you're only thirty-nine years old, if you've continued to learn and grow, others will likely start asking you to teach

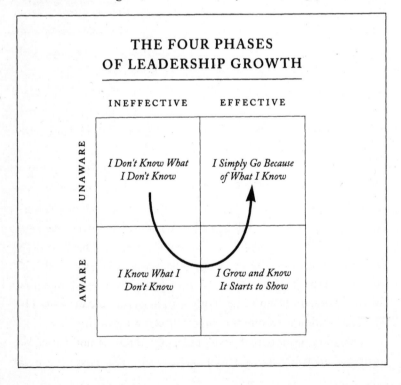

THE FOUR PHASES OF LEADERSHIP GROWTH

	INEFFECTIVE	EFFECTIVE
UNAWARE	*I Don't Know What I Don't Know*	*I Simply Go Because of What I Know*
AWARE	*I Know What I Don't Know*	*I Grow and Know It Starts to Show*

them about leadership. And some will be amazed. They'll look at each other and say, 'How did he suddenly become so wise?'

"Brian, you can be a great leader, but it won't happen in a day. Start paying the price now."

What's true for Brian is also true for you. Start developing your leadership today, and someday you will experience the effects of the Law of Process.

> *"The secret of success in life is for a man to be ready for his time when it comes."*
> —*Benjamin Disraeli*

PHASE 4—I SIMPLY GO BECAUSE OF WHAT I KNOW

When you're in phase 3, you can be pretty effective as a leader, but you have to think about every move you make. However, when you get to phase 4, your ability to lead becomes almost automatic. And that's when the payoff is larger than life. But the only way to get there is to obey the Law of Process and pay the price.

TO LEAD TOMORROW, LEARN TODAY

Leadership is developed daily, not in a day. That is the reality dictated by the Law of Process. Benjamin Disraeli asserted, "The secret of success in life is for a man to be ready for his time when it comes." What a person does on a disciplined, consistent basis gets him ready, no matter what the goal. Basketball legend Larry Bird became an outstanding free-throw shooter by practicing five hundred shots each morning before he went to school. Demosthenes of ancient Greece became the greatest orator by reciting verses with pebbles in his mouth and speaking over the roar of the waves at the seashore—and he did it despite having been born with a speech impairment. The same dedication is required for you to become a great leader.

The good news is that your leadership ability is not static. No matter where you're starting from, you can get better. That's true even for people who have stood on the world stage of leadership. While most presidents of the United States reach their peak while in office, others continue to grow and become better leaders afterward, such as former president Jimmy Carter. Some people questioned his ability to lead while in the White House. But in recent years, Carter's level of influence has continually increased. His high integrity and dedication in serving people through Habitat for Humanity and other organizations have made his influence grow. And now he has been recognized in Mali where he was knighted for his work eradicating Guinea worm disease. People now are truly impressed with his life.

FIGHTING YOUR WAY UP

There is an old saying: Champions don't become champions in the ring—they are merely recognized there. That's true. If you want to see where someone develops into a champion, look at his daily routine. Former heavyweight champ Joe Frazier stated, "You can map out a fight plan or a life plan. But when the action starts, you're down to your reflexes. That's where your road work shows. If you cheated on that in the dark of the morning, you're getting found out now under the bright lights."[3] Boxing is a good analogy for leadership development because it is all about daily preparation. Even if a person has natural talent, he has to prepare and train to become successful.

> *Champions don't become champions in the ring—they are merely recognized there.*

One of this country's greatest leaders was a fan of boxing: President Theodore Roosevelt. In fact, one of his most famous quotes uses a boxing analogy:

It is not the critic who counts, not the man who points out how the strong man stumbled, or where the doer of deeds could have done them better. The credit belongs to the man who is actually in the arena; whose face is marred by dust and sweat and blood; who strives valiantly; who errs and comes short again and again; who knows the great enthusiasms, the great devotions, and spends himself in a worthy cause; who, at best, knows in the end the triumph of high achievement; and who, at the worst, if he fails, at least fails while daring greatly, so that his place shall never be with those cold and timid souls who know neither victory nor defeat.

Roosevelt, a boxer himself, was the ultimate man of action. Not only was he an effective leader, but he was the most flamboyant of all U.S. presidents. British historian Hugh Brogan described him as "the ablest man to sit in the White House since Lincoln; the most vigorous since Jackson; the most bookish since John Quincy Adams."

A MAN OF ACTION

TR (which was Roosevelt's nickname) is remembered as an outspoken man of action and proponent of the vigorous life. While in the White House, he was known for regular boxing and judo sessions, challenging horseback rides, and long, strenuous hikes. A French ambassador who visited Roosevelt used to tell about the time that he accompanied the president on a walk through the woods. When the two men came to the banks of a stream that was too deep to cross by foot, TR stripped off his clothes and expected the dignitary to do the same so that they could swim to the other side. Nothing was an obstacle to Roosevelt.

At different times in his life, Roosevelt was a cowboy in the Wild West, an explorer and big-game hunter, and a rough-riding cavalry officer in the Spanish-American War. His enthusiasm and stamina seemed boundless. As the vice presidential candidate in 1900, he gave 673 speeches and traveled 20,000 miles while campaigning for President McKinley. And years after his presidency, while preparing to deliver a speech in Milwaukee, Roosevelt was shot in the chest by a would-be assassin. With a broken rib and a bullet in his chest, Roosevelt insisted on delivering his one-hour speech before allowing himself to be taken to the hospital.

ROOSEVELT STARTED SLOW

Of all the leaders this nation has ever had, Roosevelt was one of the toughest—both physically and mentally. But he didn't start that way. America's cowboy president was born in Manhattan to a prominent wealthy family. As a child, he was puny and very sickly. He had debilitating asthma, possessed very poor eyesight, and was painfully thin. His parents weren't sure he would survive.

When he was twelve, young Roosevelt's father told him, "You have the mind, but you have not the body, and without the help of the body the mind cannot go as far as it should. You must *make* the body." And make it he did. He lived by the Law of Process.

TR began spending time *every day* building his body as well as his mind, and he did that for the rest of his life. He worked out with weights, hiked, ice-skated, hunted, rowed, rode horseback, and boxed. In later years, Roosevelt assessed his progress, admitting that as a child he was "nervous and timid. Yet," he said, "from reading of the people I admired . . . and from knowing my father, I had a great admiration for men who were fearless and who could hold their own in the world, and I had a great desire to be like them."[4] By the time TR graduated from Harvard, he *was* like them, and he was ready to tackle the world of politics.

NO OVERNIGHT SUCCESS

Roosevelt didn't become a great leader overnight, either. His road to the presidency was one of slow, continual growth. As he served in various positions, ranging from New York City police commissioner to president of the United States, he kept learning and growing. He improved himself, and in time he became a strong leader. That was further evidence that he lived by the Law of Process.

Roosevelt's list of accomplishments is remarkable. Under his leadership, the United States emerged as a world power. He helped the country develop a first-class navy. He saw that the Panama Canal was built. He negotiated peace between Russia and Japan, winning a Nobel Peace Prize in the process. And when people questioned TR's leadership—since he had become president when McKinley was assassinated—he campaigned and was reelected by the largest majority of any president up to his time.

Ever the man of action, when Roosevelt completed his term as president in 1909, he immediately traveled to Africa where he led a scientific expedition sponsored by the Smithsonian Institution. A few years later, in 1913, he co-led a group to explore the uncharted River of Doubt in Brazil. It was a great learning adventure he said he could not pass up. "It was my last chance to be a boy," he later admitted. He was fifty-five years old.

On January 6, 1919, at his home in New York, Theodore Roosevelt died in his sleep. Then Vice President Marshall said, "Death had to take him sleeping, for if Roosevelt had been awake, there would have been a fight." When they removed him from his bed, they found a book under his pillow. Up to the very last, TR was still striving to learn and improve himself. He was still practicing the Law of Process.

If you want to be a leader, the good news is that you can do it. Everyone has the potential, but it isn't accomplished overnight. It requires perseverance. And you absolutely cannot ignore the Law of Process. Leadership doesn't develop in a day. It takes a lifetime.

THE LAW OF NAVIGATION

*Anyone Can Steer the Ship, But It
Takes a Leader to Chart the Course*

I N 1911, TWO GROUPS of explorers set off on an incredible mission. Though they used different strategies and routes, the leaders of the teams had the same goal: to be the first in history to reach the South Pole. Their stories are life-and-death illustrations of the Law of Navigation.

One of the groups was led by Norwegian explorer Roald Amundsen. Ironically, Amundsen had not originally intended to go to Antarctica. His desire was to be the first man to reach the *North* Pole. But when he discovered that Robert Peary had beaten him there, Amundsen changed his goal and headed toward the other end of the earth. North or south—he knew his planning would pay off.

AMUNDSEN CAREFULLY CHARTED HIS COURSE

Before his team ever set off, Amundsen had painstakingly planned his trip. He studied the methods of the Eskimos and other experienced Arctic travelers and determined that their best course of action would be to transport all their equipment and supplies by dogsled. When he assembled his team, he chose expert skiers and dog handlers. His strategy was simple. The dogs would do most of the work as the group traveled fifteen to twenty miles in a six-hour period each day. That would allow both the dogs and the men plenty of time to rest each day for the following day's travel.

Amundsen's forethought and attention to detail were incredible. He located and stocked supply depots all along the route. That way they would not have to carry every bit of their supplies with them the whole trip. He also equipped his people with the best gear possible. Amundsen had carefully considered every possible aspect of the journey, thought it through, and planned accordingly. And it paid off. The worst problem they experienced on the trip was an infected tooth that one man had to have extracted.

SCOTT VIOLATED THE LAW OF NAVIGATION

The other team of men was led by Robert Falcon Scott, a British naval officer who had previously done some exploring in the Antarctic area. Scott's expedition was the antithesis of Amundsen's. Instead of using dogsleds, Scott decided to use motorized sledges and ponies. Their problems began when the motors on the sledges stopped working only five days into the trip. The ponies didn't fare well either in those frigid temperatures. When they reached the foot of the Transantarctic Mountains, all of the poor animals had to be killed. As a result, the team members themselves ended up hauling the two-hundred-pound sledges. It was arduous work.

Scott hadn't given enough attention to the team's other equipment. Their clothes were so poorly designed that all the men developed frostbite. One team member required an hour every morning just to get his boots onto his swollen, gangrenous feet. And everyone became snowblind because of the inadequate goggles Scott had supplied. On top of everything else, the team was always low on food and water. That was also due to Scott's poor planning. The depots of supplies Scott established were inadequately stocked, too far apart, and often poorly marked, which made them very difficult to find. Because they were continually low on fuel to melt snow, everyone became dehydrated. Making things even worse was Scott's last-minute decision to take along a fifth man, even though they had prepared enough supplies only for four.

After covering a grueling eight hundred miles in ten weeks, Scott's exhausted group finally arrived at the South Pole on January 17, 1912. There they found the Norwegian flag flapping in the wind and a letter from Amundsen. The other well-led team had beaten them to their goal by more than a month!

IF YOU DON'T LIVE BY THE
LAW OF NAVIGATION . . .

As bad as their trip to the Pole was, that isn't the worst part of their story. The trek back was horrific. Scott and his men were starving and suffering from scurvy. But Scott, unable to navigate to the very end, was oblivious to their plight. With time running out and desperately low on food, Scott insisted that they collect thirty pounds of geological specimens to take back—more weight to be carried by the worn-out men.

Their progress became slower and slower. One member of the party sank into a stupor and died. Another, Lawrence Oates, was in terrible shape. The former army officer, who had originally been brought along to take care of the ponies, had frostbite so severe that he had trouble going on. Because he believed he was endangering the team's survival, it's said that he purposely walked out into a blizzard to relieve the group of himself as a liability. Before he left the tent and headed out into the storm, he said, "I am just going outside; I may be some time."

Scott and his final two team members made it only a little farther north before giving up. The return trip had already taken two months, and still they were 150 miles from their base camp. There they died. We know their story only because they spent their last hours writing in their diaries. Some of Scott's last words were these:

> *Because Robert Falcon Scott was unable to live by the Law of Navigation, he and his companions died by it.*

"We shall die like gentlemen. I think this will show that the Spirit of pluck and power to endure has not passed out of our race."[1] Scott had courage, but not leadership. Because he was unable to live by the Law of Navigation, he and his companions died by it.

Followers need leaders able to effectively navigate for them. When they're facing life-and-death situations, the necessity is painfully obvious. But, even when consequences aren't as serious, the need is just as great. The truth is that nearly anyone can steer the ship, but it takes a leader to chart the course. That is the Law of Navigation.

NAVIGATORS SEE THE TRIP AHEAD

General Electric chairman Jack Welch asserts, "A good leader remains focused . . . Controlling your direction is better than being controlled by it." Welch is right, but leaders who navigate do even more than control the direction in which they and their people travel. They see the whole trip in their minds before they leave the dock. They have a vision for their destination, they understand what it will take to get there, they know who they'll need on the team to be successful, and they recognize the obstacles long before they appear on the horizon. Leroy Eims, author of *Be the Leader You Were Meant to Be*, writes, "A leader is one who sees more than others see, who sees farther than others see, and who sees before others do."

The larger the organization, the more clearly the leader has to be able to see ahead. That's true because sheer size makes midcourse corrections more difficult. And if there are errors, many more people are affected than when you're traveling alone or with only a few people. The disaster shown in the recent film *Titanic* was a good example of that kind of problem. The crew could not see far enough ahead to avoid the iceberg altogether, and they could not maneu-

> *"A leader is one who sees more than others see, who sees farther than others see, and who sees before others do."*
> —*Leroy Eims*

ver enough to change course once the object was spotted because of the size of the ship, the largest built at that time. The result was that more than one thousand people lost their lives.

WHERE THE LEADER GOES . . .

First-rate navigators always have in mind that other people are depending on them and their ability to chart a good course. I read an observation by James A. Autry in *Life and Work: A Manager's Search for Meaning* that illustrates this idea. He said that occasionally you hear about the crash of four military planes flying together in a formation. The reason for the loss of all four is this: When jet fighters fly in groups of four, one pilot—the leader—designates where the team will fly. The other three planes fly on the leader's wing, watching him and following him wherever he goes. Whatever moves he makes, the rest of his team will make along with him. That's true whether he soars in the clouds or smashes into a mountaintop.

Before leaders take their people on a journey, they go through a process in order to give the trip the best chance of being a success:

NAVIGATORS DRAW ON PAST EXPERIENCE

Every past success and failure can be a source of information and wisdom—if you allow it to be. Successes teach you about yourself and what you're capable of doing with your particular gifts and talents. Failures show what kinds of wrong assumptions you've made and where your methods are flawed. If you fail to learn from your mistakes, you're going to fail again and again. That's why effective navigators start with experience. But they certainly don't end there.

NAVIGATORS LISTEN TO WHAT OTHERS HAVE TO SAY

> *No matter how much you learn from the past, it will never tell you all you need to know for the present.*

No matter how much you learn from the past, it will never tell you all you need to know for the present. That's why top-notch navigators gather information from many sources. They get ideas from members of their leadership team. They talk to the people in their organization to find out what's happening on the grassroots level. And they spend time with leaders from outside the organization who can mentor them.

NAVIGATORS EXAMINE THE CONDITIONS BEFORE MAKING COMMITMENTS

I like action, and my personality prompts me to be spontaneous. On top of that, I have reliable intuition when it comes to leadership. But I'm also conscious of my responsibilities as a leader. So before I make commitments that are going to impact my people, I take stock and thoroughly think things through. Good navigators count the cost *before* making commitments for themselves and others.

NAVIGATORS MAKE SURE THEIR CONCLUSIONS REPRESENT BOTH FAITH AND FACT

Being able to navigate for others requires a leader to possess a positive attitude. You've got to have faith that you can take your people all the way. If you can't confidently make the trip in your mind, you're not going to be able to take it in real life. On the other hand, you also have to be able to see the facts realistically. You can't minimize obstacles or rationalize your challenges. If you don't go in with your eyes wide open, you're going to get blindsided. As Bill Easum observes, "Realistic leaders are objective enough to minimize illusions. They understand that self-deception can cost them their vision." Sometimes it's difficult balancing optimism and realism, intuition and planning, faith and fact. But that's what it takes to be effective as a navigating leader.

> *It's difficult balancing optimism and realism, intuition and planning, faith and fact. But that's what it takes to be effective as a navigating leader.*

A LESSON IN NAVIGATION

I remember the first time I really understood the importance of the Law of Navigation. I was twenty-eight years old, and I was leading Faith Memorial in Lancaster, Ohio, my second church. Before my arrival there in 1972, the church had experienced a decade-long plateau in its growth. But by 1975, our attendance had gone from four hundred to more than one thousand. I knew we could keep growing and reach more people, but only if we built a new auditorium.

> *If the leader can't navigate the people through rough waters, he is liable to sink the ship.*

The good news was that I already had some experience in building and relocation because I had taken my first church through the process. The bad news was that the first one was really small in comparison to the second one. To give you an idea of the difference, the changing room in the nursery in Lancaster was going to be larger than the whole sanctuary in the original building of my first church!

It was going to be a multimillion-dollar project more than twenty times larger than my first one. But even that was not the greatest obstacle. Right before I came on board at Faith Memorial, there had been a huge battle over another building proposal, and the debate had been vocal, divisive, and bitter. For that reason, I knew that I would experience genuine opposition to my leadership for the first time. There were rough waters ahead, and if I as the leader didn't navigate us well, I could sink the ship.

CHARTING THE COURSE
WITH A NAVIGATION STRATEGY

At that time I developed a strategy that I have since used repeatedly in my leadership. I wrote it as an acrostic so that I would always be able to remember it:

Predetermine a Course of Action.
Lay Out Your Goals.
Adjust Your Priorities.
Notify Key Personnel.

Allow Time for Acceptance.
Head into Action.
Expect Problems.
Always Point to the Successes.
Daily Review Your Plan.

That became my blueprint as I prepared to navigate for my people.

Back then, I knew exactly what our course of action needed to be. If we were going to keep growing, we needed to build a new auditorium. I had looked at every possible alternative, and I knew that was our only viable solution. My goal was to design and build the facility, pay for it in ten years, and unify all the people in the process. I also knew our biggest adjustment would come in the area of finances, since it would turn our current budget upside down.

I started preparing for the congregational meeting. I scheduled it a couple of months ahead to give me time to get everything ready. The first thing I did was direct our board members and a group of key financial leaders to conduct a twenty-year analysis of our growth and financial patterns. It covered the previous ten years and projections for the next ten years. Based on that, we determined the requirements of the facility. Then we formulated a ten-year budget that carefully explained how we would handle the financing. I also asked that all of the information we were gathering be put into a twenty-page report that I intended to give to the members of the congregation. I knew that major barriers to successful planning are fear of change, ignorance, uncertainty about the future, and lack of imagination. I was going to do everything I could to prevent those factors from hindering us.

> *Major barriers to successful planning are fear of change, ignorance, uncertainty about the future, and lack of imagination.*

My next step was to notify the key leaders. I started with the ones who had the most influence, meeting with them individually and sometimes in small groups. Over the course of several weeks, I met with about a hundred leaders. I cast the vision for them and fielded their questions. And when I could sense that a person was hesitant about the project, I planned to meet individually with him again. Then I allowed time for the rest of the people to be influenced by those leaders and for acceptance to develop among the congregation.

When the time rolled around for the congregational meeting, we were ready to head into action. I took two hours to present the project to the people. I handed out my twenty-page report with the floor plans, financial analysis, and budgets. I tried to answer every question the people would have before they had a chance to ask it. I also asked some of the most influential people in the congregation to speak.

I had expected some opposition, but when I opened the floor for questions, I was shocked. There were only two questions: One person wanted to know about the placement of the building's water fountains, and the other asked about the number of rest rooms.

> *The secret to the Law of Navigation is preparation.*

That was when I knew we had navigated the tricky waters successfully. When it was time for the motion asking everyone to vote, the church's most influential layperson made it. And I had arranged for the leader who had previously opposed building to second the motion. When the final count was tallied, 98 percent of the people had voted in favor.

Once we had navigated through that phase, the rest of the project wasn't difficult. I continually kept the vision in front of the people by giving them good news reports to acknowledge our successes. And I periodically reviewed our plans and their results to make sure we were on track. The course had been charted. All we had to do was steer the ship.

> *It's not the size of the project that determines its acceptance, support, and success. It's the size of the leader.*

That was a wonderful learning experience for me. Above everything else I found out that the secret to the Law of Navigation is preparation. When you prepare well, you convey confidence and trust to the people. Lack of preparation has the opposite effect. You see, it's not the size of the project that determines its acceptance, support, and success. It's the size of the leader. That's why I say that anyone can *steer* the ship, but it takes a leader to chart the course. Leaders who are good navigators are capable of taking their people just about anywhere.

5

THE LAW OF E. F. HUTTON

When the Real Leader Speaks, People Listen

YOUNG, INEXPERIENCED LEADERS often walk confidently into a room full of people only to discover that they have totally misjudged the leadership dynamics of the situation. I know that's happened to me! But when it did, it usually didn't take me very long to recognize my blunder. That was the case when I presided over my very first board meeting as a young leader. It occurred in the first church I led in rural Indiana, right after I graduated from college at age twenty-two. I hadn't been at the church for much more than a month, and I was leading a group of people whose average age was about fifty. Most of the people in the meeting had been at that church longer than I'd been alive.

I went into the meeting with no preconceptions, no agenda—and no clue. I figured that I was the appointed leader and just assumed everyone would follow me because of that. With all the wisdom and knowledge of my two decades of life experience, I opened the meeting and asked whether anyone had an issue to discuss.

There was a brief pause as I looked around the table, and then a man in his sixties named Claude cleared his throat and said, "I've got something."

"Go right ahead, Claude," I said.

"Well," he said, "I've noticed lately that the piano seems to be out of tune when it's played in the service."

"You know, I've noticed the same thing," said one of the other board members.

"I make a motion that we spend the money to get a piano tuner to come out from Louisville and take care of it," said Claude.

"Hey, that's a great idea," everyone at the table started saying.

"I second the motion," said Benny, the board member sitting next to Claude.

> *The* real
> *leader holds the*
> *power, not just*
> *the position.*

"That's great," I said. "Does anybody else have anything?"

"Yep," said Claude, "I noticed the other day that there's a pane of glass in one of the Sunday school rooms that's busted. I've got a piece a glass out at the farm that would fit that. Benny, you're a pretty good glazer. How about you put that glass in."

"Sure, Claude," said Benny, "I'd be glad to."

"Good. There's one other thing," said Claude. "This year's picnic. I was thinking maybe this time we ought to have it down by the lake. I think it would be good for the kids."

"Oh, that would be perfect. What a good idea!" everyone started saying.

"Let's make it official," Benny said.

As everyone nodded agreement, we all waited to see if Claude had anything else to say.

"That's all I've got," said Claude. "Pastor, why don't you close us in prayer." And that's what I did. That was pretty much the whole content of my first board meeting. And it was also the day I realized who the real leader in that church was. I held the position, but

Claude had the power. That's when I discovered the Law of E. F. Hutton.

You've probably heard of E. F. Hutton, the financial services company. Years ago, their motto was, "When E. F. Hutton speaks, people listen." Maybe you remember their old television commercials. The setting was typically a busy restaurant or other public place. Two people would be talking about financial matters, and the first person would repeat something his broker had said concerning a certain investment. The second person would say, "Well, my broker is E. F. Hutton, and E. F. Hutton says . . ." At that point every single person in the bustling restaurant would stop dead in his tracks, turn, and listen to what the man was about to say. That's why I call this leadership truth the Law of E. F. Hutton. Because when the *real* leader speaks, people do listen.

WHAT COULD I DO?

After my first board meeting, I had to determine how I was going to handle the situation in my church. I had several options. For example, I could have insisted on my right to be in charge. I've seen a lot of positional leaders do that over the years. They tell their people something like this: "Hey, wait! I'm the leader. You're supposed to follow me." But that doesn't work. People might be polite to you, but they won't really follow. It's similar to something former British prime minister Margaret Thatcher once said: "Being in power is like being a lady. If you have to tell people you are, you aren't."

> *"Being in power is like being a lady. If you have to tell people you are, you aren't."*
> —*Margaret Thatcher*

Another option would have been to try to push Claude out as the leader. But how do you think that would have turned out? He was more than twice my age, he had lived in that area his whole life, and he was respected by everybody in the community. He was a member of that church before I got there, and everybody knew that he would be there long after I left.

I pursued a third option. By the time the next board meeting was ready to roll around, I had a list of items that I knew needed to be accomplished at the church. So about a week before we were scheduled to meet, I called Claude and asked him if I could come out to the farm and spend some time with him. As we did chores together throughout the day, he and I talked.

"Claude," I said, "you know, I've noticed that the front door on the church is cracked and peeling. It would look terrible to any new people coming to the church for the first time. Do you think we could do something about that?"

"Sure," said Claude, "that would be no problem."

I continued, "I went down into the basement the other day. Did you know there's water down in there? Shoot, there are frogs hopping around down there, tadpoles swimming, and crawdads crawling. What do you think we ought to do?"

"Well, John," Claude said, "I think we ought to have a work day and get that basement all cleaned out."

"That's a great idea," I said. "Would you bring that up at our next board meeting?"

"I sure will."

"There's another thing that's been worrying me," I continued. "Right now we've got only three rooms in the building besides the auditorium. One is being used as a storage room for a bunch of junk. The other two are for Sunday school, but one of those classes has an awful lot of kids and is getting pretty full."

"Don't say another word," said Claude. "We'll get that room all cleaned out."

"Oh, that would be great. Thank you, Claude."

At the next board meeting, when I called for new business, Claude said, "You know, I think it's about time for us to have a work day around here."

"That's a great idea," everyone around the table started saying.

"We'll have it a week from Saturday," said Claude. "I'll bring my truck, and, Benny, you bring yours too. We're going to do some painting, clean out that basement, and get the junk out of that storage room. We need it for a new Sunday school class." Then he turned to one of the board members and said, "And Sister Maxine, you're going to teach it."

> *If you see a disparity between who's leading the meeting and who's leading the people, then the person running the meeting is not the real leader.*

"I second that," said Benny, and that was it.

From then on, if I wanted to accomplish anything at that church, I just went out to the farm and did chores with Claude. I could always count on him to bring those things before the people, and whenever Claude spoke, people listened.

THE EYES HAVE IT

Once you learn the Law of E. F. Hutton, you'll never have trouble figuring out who the real leader is in just about any situation. For example, go to a meeting with a group of people you've never met before and watch them for five minutes. You'll know who the leader is. When somebody asks a question, who do people watch? Who do they wait to hear? The person they look to is the real leader.

Try it. The next time you're in a meeting, look around you. See if you notice a difference between these two kinds of leaders:

POSITIONAL LEADERS	REAL LEADERS
Speak first	*Speak later*
Need the influence of the real leader to get things done	*Need only their own influence to get things done*
Influence only the other positional leaders	*Influence everyone in the room*

If you see a disparity between who's leading the *meeting* and who's leading the *people*, then the person running the meeting is not the real leader.

> **The real test of leadership isn't where you start out. It's where you end up.**

I have never been the real leader at any job when I started it, other than at the companies I've founded. When I took that first position in Hillham, Indiana, Claude was the leader. In my second church in Ohio, the real leader was a man named Jim. And when I went to Skyline in San Diego, the staff first followed Steve, not me. So if you're starting in a new position and you're not the leader, don't let it bother you. The real test of leadership isn't where you start out. It's where you end up.

WILL THE REAL LEADER PLEASE STAND UP?

Many years ago, there was a game show called *To Tell the Truth*. Here's how it worked. At the opening of the show, three contestants claimed to be the same person. One of them was telling the truth; the other two were actors. A panel of celebrity judges took turns asking the three people questions, and when time was up, each panelist guessed which person was the real truth-teller. Many times, the actors bluffed well enough to fool the panelists and the members of the audience.

When it comes to identifying a real leader, that task can be much easier—if you remember what you're looking for. Don't listen to the claims of the person professing to be the leader. Instead, watch the reactions of the people around him. The proof of leadership is found in the followers.

Think about the reactions certain people get when they speak. When Alan Greenspan speaks before Congress, everybody listens. When he prepares to make a statement on lending rates, the entire financial community stops what it's doing. It's really a lot like the old E. F. Hutton commercials. When Martin Luther King Jr. was alive, he got an incredible amount of respect. No matter where or when he spoke, people—black and white—listened. Today,

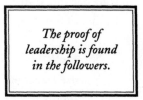

The proof of leadership is found in the followers.

Billy Graham gets a similar kind of respect because of his unquestionable integrity and lifetime of service. For nearly fifty years, his advice has been heeded by world leaders. Every president of the United States since Harry Truman has sought his leadership and wise counsel.

The Law of E. F. Hutton reveals itself in just about every kind of situation. I read a story about former NBA player Larry Bird that illustrates it well. During the final seconds of an especially tense game, Boston Celtics coach K. C. Jones called a time-out. As he gathered the players together at courtside, he diagrammed a play, only to have Bird say, "Get the ball out to me and get everyone out of my way."

Jones responded, "I'm the coach, and I'll call the plays!" Then he turned to the other players and said, "Get the ball to Larry and get out of his way."[1] It just shows that when the real leader speaks, people listen.

PEOPLE BECOME REAL LEADERS BECAUSE OF . . .

How do the real leaders *become* the real leaders within groups? As I explained in the chapter on the Law of Process, leadership doesn't develop in just a day. Neither does a person's recognition as a leader. Over the course of time, seven key areas reveal themselves in leader's lives that cause them to step forward as leaders:

1. CHARACTER—WHO THEY ARE

True leadership always begins with the inner person. That's why someone like Billy Graham is able to draw more and more followers to him as time goes by. People can sense the depth of his character.

2. RELATIONSHIPS—WHO THEY KNOW

You're a leader only if you have followers, and that always requires the development of relationships—the deeper the relationships, the stronger the potential for leadership. Each time I entered a new leadership position, I immediately started building relationships. Build enough of the right kinds of relationships with the right people, and you can become the real leader in an organization.

3. KNOWLEDGE—WHAT THEY KNOW

Information is vital to a leader. You need a grasp of the facts, an understanding of the factors involved, and a vision for the future. Knowledge alone won't make someone a leader, but without it, he can't become one. I always spent a lot of time doing homework before I tried to take the lead in an organization.

4. INTUITION—WHAT THEY FEEL

Leadership requires more than just a command of data. It demands an ability to deal with numerous intangibles (as I explain in the chapter on the Law of Intuition).

5. EXPERIENCE—WHERE THEY'VE BEEN

The greater the challenges you've faced in the past, the more likely followers are to give you a chance. Experience doesn't guarantee credibility, but it encourages people to give you a chance to prove that you are capable.

6. PAST SUCCESS—WHAT THEY'VE DONE

Nothing speaks to followers like a good track record. When I went to my first church, I had no track record. I couldn't point to past successes to help people believe in me. But by the time I went to my second church, I had a few. Every time I extended myself, took a risk, and succeeded, followers had another reason to trust my leadership ability—and to listen to what I had to say.

7. ABILITY—WHAT THEY CAN DO

The bottom line for followers is what a leader is capable of. Ultimately, that's the reason people will listen to you and acknowledge you as their leader. As soon as they no longer believe you can deliver, they will stop listening.

WHEN SHE SPOKE . . .

Once you have a handle on the Law of E. F. Hutton, you understand that people listen to what someone has to say not necessarily because of the truth being communicated in the message, but because of their respect for the speaker.

I was reminded of this again recently when I read something about Mother Teresa. When most people think about her they envision a frail little woman dedicated to serving the poorest of the poor. That she was. But she was

> *People listen not necessarily because of the truth being communicated in the message, but because of their respect for the speaker.*

also a real leader. Lucinda Vardey, who worked with Mother Teresa on the book *The Simple Path*, described the nun as "the quintessential, energetic entrepreneur, who has perceived a need and done something about it, built an organization against all odds, formulated its constitution, and sent out branches all over the world."

The organization Mother Teresa founded and led is called the Missionaries of Charity. While other vocational orders in the Catholic Church declined, hers grew rapidly, reaching more than four thousand members during her lifetime (not including numerous volunteers). Under her direction, her followers served in twenty-five countries on five continents. In Calcutta alone, she established a children's home, a center for people with leprosy, a home for people who were dying and destitute, and a home for people suffering with tuberculosis or mental disorders. That kind of organizational building can be accomplished only by a true leader.

Author and former presidential speechwriter Peggy Noonan wrote about a speech Mother Teresa gave at the National Prayer Breakfast in 1994. Noonan said,

> The Washington establishment was there, plus a few thousand born-again Christians, orthodox Catholics, and Jews. Mother Teresa spoke of God, of love, of families. She said we must love one another and care for one another. There were great purrs of agreement.
>
> But as the speech continued, it became more pointed. She spoke of unhappy parents in old people's homes who are "hurt because they are forgotten." She asked, "Are we willing to give until it hurts in order to be with our families, or do we put our own interests first?"
>
> The baby boomers in the audience began to shift in their seats. And she continued. "I feel that the greatest destroyer of peace today is abortion," she said, and told them why, in uncom-

promising terms. For about 1.3 seconds there was silence, then applause swept the room. But not everyone clapped; the President and First Lady, the Vice President and Mrs. Gore looked like seated statues at Madame Tussaud's moving not a muscle. Mother Teresa didn't stop there either. When she was finished, there was almost no one she hadn't offended.[2]

If just about any other person in the world had made those statements, people's reactions would have been openly hostile. They would have booed, jeered, or stormed out. But the speaker was Mother Teresa. She was probably the most respected person on the planet at that time. So everyone listened to what she had to say, even though many of them violently disagreed with it. In fact, *every time* that Mother Teresa spoke, people listened. Why? She was a real leader, and when the real leader speaks, people listen.

So I must ask you this: How do people react when you communicate? When you speak, do people listen—I mean *really* listen? Or do they wait to hear what someone else has to say before they act? You can find out a lot about your level of leadership if you have the courage to ask and answer that question. That's the power of the Law of E. F. Hutton.

6

THE LAW OF SOLID GROUND

Trust Is the Foundation of Leadership

I PERSONALLY LEARNED THE power of the Law of Solid Ground in the fall of 1989. It happened during a very busy time when I was the senior pastor at Skyline Church in San Diego. Every year, we created and performed a major Christmas production. It was a really big deal. The cast included more than 300 people. The staging was elaborate—on the level of most professional productions. Each year more than 25,000 people saw the show, and it had become a San Diego tradition, having been produced annually for more than two decades.

That year the fall season was very hectic for me. We had several new programs starting at the church. Preparations for the Christmas show were in full swing. In addition, I was doing quite a bit of speaking and traveling around the country. And because I was so busy, I let my choleric nature get the better of me and made a big mistake. I very quickly made three major decisions and implemented them without providing the right kind of leadership. In one week, I changed some components of the Christmas show, I permanently discontinued our Sunday evening service, and I fired a staff member.

IT WASN'T THE DECISIONS— IT WAS THE LEADERSHIP

What's interesting is that none of my three decisions was wrong. The change in the Christmas program was beneficial. The Sunday evening service, though enjoyed by some of the older members of the congregation, wasn't building the church or serving a need that wasn't already being met elsewhere. And the particular staff member I fired had to go, and it was important that I not delay in dismissing him.

My mistake was the way I made those three decisions. Because everything in the church was going so well, I thought I could act on the decisions without taking everyone through the deliberate steps needed to process them. Ordinarily, I would gather my leaders, cast vision for them, answer questions, and guide them through the issues. Then I would give them time to exert their influence with the next level of leaders in the church. And finally, once the timing was right, I would make a general announcement to all, letting them know about the decisions, giving them plenty of reassurance, and encouraging them to be a part of the new vision. But I didn't do any of those things, and I should have known better.

THE RESULT WAS MISTRUST

It wasn't long afterward that I began to sense unrest among the people. I also heard some rumblings. At first, my attitude was that everyone should get over it and move on. But then I realized that the problem wasn't them. It was me. I had handled things badly. And on top of that, my attitude wasn't very positive—not good when you're the guy who wrote a book called *The Winning Attitude!* That's when

I realized that I had broken the Law of Solid Ground. For the first time in my life, my people didn't completely trust me.

As soon as I realized I was wrong, I publicly apologized to my people and asked for their forgiveness. Your people know when you make mistakes. The real question is whether you're going to 'fess up. If you do, you can often quickly regain their trust. That's what happened with me once I apologized. And from then on, I made sure to do things right. I learned firsthand that when it comes to leadership, you just can't take shortcuts, no matter how long you've been leading your people.

> *When it comes to leadership, you just can't take shortcuts, no matter how long you've been leading your people.*

It didn't take long for me to get back onto solid ground with everyone. As I've explained in *Developing the Leader Within You*, a leader's history of successes and failures makes a big difference in his credibility. It's a little like earning and spending pocket change. Each time you make a good leadership decision, it puts change into your pocket. Each time you make a poor one, you have to pay out some of your change to the people.

Every leader has a certain amount of change in his pocket when he starts in a new leadership position. From then on, he either builds up his change or pays it out. If he makes one bad decision after another, he keeps paying out change. Then one day, after making one last bad decision, he is going to reach into his pocket and realize he is out of change. It doesn't even matter if the blunder was big or small. When you're out of change, you're out as the leader.

A leader who keeps making good decisions and keeps recording wins for the organization builds up his change. Then even if he makes a huge blunder, he can still have plenty of change left over. That's the kind of history I had at Skyline, which is why I was able to rebuild trust with the people very quickly.

TRUST IS THE FOUNDATION OF LEADERSHIP

Trust is the foundation of leadership. To build trust, a leader must exemplify these qualities: competence, connection, and character. People will forgive occasional mistakes based on ability, especially if they can see that you're still growing as a leader. But they won't trust someone who has slips in character. In that area, even occasional lapses are lethal. All effective leaders know this truth. PepsiCo chairman and CEO Craig Weatherup acknowledges, "People will tolerate honest mistakes, but if you violate their trust you will find it very difficult to ever regain their confidence. That is one reason that you need to treat trust as your most precious asset. You may fool your boss but you can never fool your colleagues or subordinates."

> *To build trust, a leader must exemplify competence, connection, and character.*

General H. Norman Schwarzkopf points to the significance of character: "Leadership is a potent combination of strategy and character. But if you must be without one, be without strategy." Character and leadership credibility always go hand in hand. Anthony Harrigan, president of the U.S. Business and Industrial Council, said,

> The role of character always has been the key factor in the rise and fall of nations. And one can be sure that America is no exception to this rule of history. We won't survive as a country because we are smarter or more sophisticated but because we are—we hope—stronger inwardly. In short, character is the only effective bulwark against internal and external forces that lead to a country's disintegration or collapse.

Character makes trust possible. And trust makes leadership possible. That is the Law of Solid Ground.

CHARACTER COMMUNICATES

Whenever you lead people, it's as if they consent to take a journey with you. The way that trip is going to turn out is predicted by your character. With good character, the longer the trip is, the better it seems. But if your character is flawed, the longer the trip is, the worse it gets. Why? Because no one enjoys spending time with someone he doesn't trust.

Character communicates many things to followers:

CHARACTER COMMUNICATES CONSISTENCY

Leaders without inner strength can't be counted on day after day because their ability to perform changes constantly. NBA great Jerry West commented, "You can't get too much done in life if you only work on the days when you feel good." If your people don't know what to expect from you as a leader, at some point they won't look to you for leadership.

> *Character makes trust possible. And trust makes leadership possible. That is the Law of Solid Ground.*

Think about what happened in the late 1980s. Several high-profile Christian leaders stumbled and fell due to moral issues. That lack of consistency compromised their ability to lead their people. In fact, it gave a black eye to every pastor across the nation because it caused people to become suspicious of all church leaders, regardless of their personal track records. The flawed character of those fallen leaders destroyed the foundation for their leadership.

When I think of leaders who epitomize consistency of character, the first person who comes to mind is Billy Graham. Regardless of personal religious beliefs, everybody trusts him. Why? Because he has modeled high character for more than half a century. He lives out his values every day. He never makes a commitment unless he is going to keep it. And he goes out of his way to personify integrity.

CHARACTER COMMUNICATES POTENTIAL

John Morley observed, "No man can climb out beyond the limitations of his own character." That's especially true when it comes to leadership. Take, for instance, the case of NHL coach Mike Keenan. As of mid-1997, he had a noteworthy record of professional hockey victories: the fifth greatest number of regular-season wins, the third greatest number of play-off victories, six division titles, four NHL finals appearances, and one Stanley Cup.

> "No man can climb out beyond the limitations of his own character."
> —John Morley

Yet despite those commendable credentials, Keenan was unable to stay with a single team for any length of time. In eleven and a half seasons, he coached four different teams. And after his stint with the fourth team—the St. Louis Blues—he was unable to land a job for a long time. Why? Sportswriter E. M. Swift said of Keenan, "The reluctance to hire Keenan is *easily* explicable. Everywhere he has been, he has alienated players and management."[1] Evidently, his players didn't trust him. Neither did the owners, who were benefiting from seeing their teams win. It seems he kept violating the Law of Solid Ground.

Craig Weatherup explains, "You don't build trust by talking about it. You build it by achieving results, always with integrity and in a manner that shows real personal regard for the people with whom you work."[2] When a leader's character is strong, people trust him, and they trust in his ability to release their potential. That not only gives followers hope for the future, but it also promotes a strong belief in themselves and their organization.

CHARACTER COMMUNICATES RESPECT

When you don't have strength within, you can't earn respect without. And respect is absolutely essential for lasting leadership. How do leaders earn respect? By making sound decisions, admitting their mistakes, and putting what's best for their followers and the organization ahead of their personal agendas.

Several years ago, a movie was made about the Fifty-fourth Massachusetts Infantry regiment and its colonel, Robert Gould Shaw. The film was called *Glory,* and though some of its plot was fictionalized, the Civil War story of Shaw's journey with his men—and of the respect he earned from them—was real.

The movie recounted the formation of this first unit in the Union army composed of African-American soldiers. Shaw, a white officer, took command of the regiment, oversaw recruiting, selected the (white) officers, equipped the men, and trained them as soldiers. He drove them hard, knowing that their performance in battle would either vindicate or condemn the value of black people as soldiers and citizens in the minds of many white

> *How do leaders earn respect? By making sound decisions, admitting their mistakes, and putting what's best for their followers and the organization ahead of their personal agendas.*

Northerners. In the process, both the soldiers and Shaw earned one another's respect.

A few months after their training was complete, the men of the Fifty-fourth got the opportunity to prove themselves in the Union assault on Confederate Fort Wagner in South Carolina. Shaw's biographer Russell Duncan said of the attack: "With a final admonition to 'prove yourselves men,' Shaw positioned himself in front and ordered, 'forward.' Years later, one soldier remembered that the regiment fought hard because Shaw was in front, not behind."

Almost half of the six hundred men from the Fifty-fourth who fought that day were wounded, captured, or killed. Though they fought valiantly, they were unable to take Fort Wagner. And Shaw, who had courageously led his men to the top of the fort's parapet in the first assault, was killed along with his men.

Shaw's actions on that final day solidified the respect his men already had for him. Two weeks after the battle, Albanus Fisher, a sergeant in the Fifty-fourth, said, "I still feel more Eager for the struggle than I ever yet have, for I now wish to have Revenge for our galant Curnel [*sic*]."[3] J. R. Miller once observed, "The only thing that walks back from the tomb with the mourners and refuses to be buried is the character of a man. This is true. What a man is survives him. It can never be buried." Shaw's character, strong to the last, had communicated a level of respect to his men that lived beyond him.

> "The only thing that walks back from the tomb with the mourners and refuses to be buried is the character of a man. This is true. What a man is survives him. It can never be buried."
> —J. R. Miller

A leader's good character builds trust among his followers. But when a leader breaks trust, he forfeits his ability to lead. That's the Law of Solid Ground. I was again reminded of this while listening to a lesson taught by my friend Bill Hybels. Four times a year, he and I teach a seminar called Leading and Communicating to Change Lives. Bill was conducting a session titled "Lessons from a Leadership Nightmare," and he shared observations and insights on some of the leadership mistakes made by Robert McNamara and the Johnson administration during the Vietnam War: the administration's inability to prioritize multiple challenges, its acceptance of faulty assumptions, and Johnson's failure to face serious staff conflicts. But in my opinion, the greatest insight Bill shared during that talk concerned the failure of American leaders, including McNamara, to face and publicly admit the terrible mistakes they had made concerning the war in Vietnam. Their actions broke trust with the American people, and because of that, they violated the Law of Solid Ground. The United States has been suffering from the repercussions ever since.

AN INHERITED POLICY BECOMES
A LEADERSHIP-SHATTERING PROBLEM

Vietnam was already at war when President Kennedy and Robert McNamara, his secretary of defense, took office in January of 1961. The Vietnam region had been a battleground for decades, and the United States got involved in the mid-1950s when President Eisenhower sent a small number of U.S. troops to Vietnam as advisors. When Kennedy took office, he continued Eisenhower's policy. It was always his intention to let the South Vietnamese fight and win their own war, but over time, the United States became increasingly involved. Before the war was over, more than half a million American troops at a time served in Vietnam.

If you remember those war years, you may be surprised to know that American support for the war was very strong even as the number of troops being sent overseas rapidly increased and the casualties mounted. By 1966, more than two hundred thousand Americans had been sent to Vietnam, yet two-thirds of all Americans surveyed by Louis Harris believed that Vietnam was the place where the United States should "stand and fight communism." And most people expressed the belief that the U.S. should stay until the fight was finished.

FIRST TRUST, THEN SUPPORT

But support didn't continue for long. The Vietnam War was being handled very badly. On top of that, our leaders continued the war even after they realized that we couldn't win it. But the worst mistake of all was that McNamara and President Johnson weren't honest with the American people about it. That broke the Law of Solid Ground, and it ultimately destroyed the administration's leadership.

In his book *In Retrospect,* McNamara recounts that he repeatedly minimized American losses and told only half-truths about the war. For example, he says, "Upon my return to Washington [from Saigon] on December 21, [1963,] I was less than candid when I reported to the press . . . I said, 'We observed the results of a very substantial increase in Vietcong activity' (true); but I then added, 'We reviewed the plans of the South Vietnamese and we have every reason to believe they will be successful' (an overstatement at best)."

For a while, nobody questioned McNamara's statements because there was no reason to mistrust the country's leadership. But in time, people recognized that his words and the facts weren't matching up. And that's when the American public began to lose faith. Years later, McNamara admitted his failure: "We of the Kennedy and Johnson administrations who participated in the decisions on Vietnam acted according to what we thought were the principles and traditions of this nation. We made our decisions in light of those values. Yet we were wrong, terribly wrong."[4]

BY THEN, IT WAS TOO LATE

Many would argue that McNamara's admission came thirty years and fifty-eight thousand lives too late. The cost of Vietnam was high, and not just in human lives. As the American people's trust in their leaders eroded, so did their willingness to follow them. Protests led to open rebellion and to societywide turmoil. The era that had begun with the hope and idealism characterized by John F. Kennedy ultimately ended with the mistrust and cynicism associated with Richard Nixon.

Whenever a leader breaks the Law of Solid Ground, he pays a price in his leadership. McNamara and President Johnson lost the trust of the American people, and their ability to lead suffered as a result. Eventually, McNamara resigned as secretary of defense. Johnson, the consummate politician, recognized his weakened position, and he didn't run for reelection. But the repercussions of broken trust didn't end there. The American people's distrust for politicians has continued to this day, and it is still growing.

No leader can break trust with his people and expect to keep influencing them. Trust is the foundation of leadership. Violate the Law of Solid Ground, and you're through as a leader.

THE LAW OF RESPECT

*People Naturally Follow Leaders
Stronger Than Themselves*

I F YOU HAD SEEN HER, your first reaction might not have been respect. She wasn't a very impressive-looking woman—just a little over five feet tall, in her late thirties, with dark brown weathered skin. She couldn't read or write. The clothes she wore were coarse and worn. When she smiled, people could see that her top two front teeth were missing.

She lived alone. The story was that she had abandoned her husband when she was twenty-nine. She gave him no warning. One day he woke up, and she was gone. She talked to him only once after that, years later, and she never mentioned his name again afterward.

Her employment was intermittent. Most of the time she took domestic jobs in small hotels: scrubbing floors, making up rooms, and cooking. But just about every spring and fall she would disappear from her place of employment, come back broke, and work again to scrape together what little money she could. When she was present on the job, she worked hard and seemed physically tough, but she also was known to have bouts where she would suddenly fall asleep—

some coming in the middle of a conversation. She attributed her affliction to a blow to the head she had taken during a teenage fight.

Who would respect a woman like that? The answer is the more than three hundred slaves who followed her to freedom out of the South—they recognized and respected her leadership. So did just about every abolitionist in New England. The year was 1857. The woman's name was Harriet Tubman.

A LEADER BY ANY OTHER NAME

While she was only in her thirties, Harriet Tubman came to be called Moses because of her ability to go into the land of captivity and bring so many of her people out of slavery's bondage. Tubman started life as a slave. She was born in 1820 and grew up in the farmland of Maryland. When she was thirteen, she received the blow to her head that troubled her all her life. She was in a store, and a white overseer demanded her assistance so that he could beat an escaping slave. When she refused and blocked the overseer's way, the man threw a two-pound weight that hit Tubman in the head. She nearly died, and her recovery took months.

At age twenty-four, she married John Tubman, a free black man. But when she talked to him about escaping to freedom in the North, he wouldn't hear of it. He said that if she tried to leave, he'd turn her in. When she resolved to take her chances and go north in 1849, she did so alone, without a word to him. Her first biographer, Sarah Bradford, said that Tubman told her: "I had reasoned this out in my mind: there was one of two things I had a *right* to, liberty or death. If I could not have one, I would have the other, for no man should take me alive. I should fight for my liberty as my strength lasted, and when the time came for me to go, the Lord would let them take me."

Tubman made her way to Philadelphia, Pennsylvania, via the Underground Railroad, a secret network of free blacks, white abolitionists, and Quakers who helped escaping slaves on the run. Though free herself, she vowed to return to Maryland and bring her family out. In 1850, she made her first return trip as an Underground Railroad "conductor"—someone who retrieved and guided out slaves with the assistance of sympathizers along the way.

A LEADER OF STEEL

Each summer and winter, Tubman worked as a domestic, scraping together the funds she needed to make return trips to the South. And every spring and fall, she risked her life by going south and returning with more people. She was fearless, and her leadership was unshakable. It was extremely dangerous work, and when people in her charge wavered, she was strong as steel. Tubman knew escaped slaves who returned would be beaten and tortured until they gave information about those who had helped them. So she never allowed any people she was guiding to give up. "Dead folks tell no tales," she would tell a faint-hearted slave as she put a loaded pistol to his head. "You go on or die!"

Between 1850 and 1860, Harriet Tubman guided out more than three hundred people, including many of her own family members. She made nineteen trips in all and was very proud of the fact that she never once lost a single person under her care. "I never ran my train off the track," she said, "and I never lost a passenger." Southern whites put a $12,000 price on her head—a fortune. Southern blacks simply called her Moses. By the start of the Civil War, she had brought more people out of slavery than any other American in history—black or white, male or female.

INCREASING RESPECT

Tubman's reputation and influence commanded respect, and not just among slaves who dreamed of gaining their freedom. Influential

Northerners of both races sought her out. She spoke at rallies and in homes throughout Philadelphia, Pennsylvania; Boston, Massachusetts; St. Catharines, Canada; and Auburn, New York, where she eventually settled. People of prominence sought her out, such as Senator William Seward, who later became Abraham Lincoln's secretary of state, and outspoken abolitionist and former slave Frederick Douglass. Tubman's advice and leadership were also requested by John Brown, the famed revolutionary abolitionist. Brown always referred to the former slave as "General Tubman," and he was quoted as saying she "was a better officer than most whom he had seen, and could command an army as successfully as she had led her small parties of fugitives."[1] That is the essence of the Law of Respect.

A TEST OF LEADERSHIP

Harriet Tubman would appear to be an unlikely candidate for leadership because the deck was certainly stacked against her. She was un-educated. She lived in a culture that didn't respect African-Americans. And she labored in a country where women didn't have the right to vote yet. Despite her circumstances, she became an incredible leader. The reason is simple: People naturally follow leaders stronger than themselves. Everyone who came in contact with her recognized her strong leadership ability and felt compelled to follow her. That's how the Law of Respect works.

> *When people respect someone as a person, they admire her. When they respect her as a friend, they love her. When they respect her as a leader, they follow her.*

IT'S NOT A GUESSING GAME

People don't follow others by accident. They follow individuals whose leadership they respect. Someone who is an 8 in leadership (on a scale from 1 to 10, with 10 being the strongest) doesn't go out and look for a 6 to follow—he naturally follows a 9 or 10. The less skilled follow the more highly skilled and gifted. Occasionally, a strong leader may choose to follow someone weaker than himself. But when that happens, it's for a reason. For example, the stronger leader may do it out of respect for the person's office or past accomplishments. Or he may be following the chain of command. In general, though, followers are attracted to people who are better leaders than themselves. That is the Law of Respect.

> *The more leadership ability a person has, the more quickly he recognizes leadership—or its lack—in others.*

When people get together for the first time as a group, take a look at what happens. As they start interacting, the leaders in the group immediately take charge. They think in terms of the direction they desire to go and who they want to take with them. At first, people may make tentative moves in several different directions, but after the people get to know one another, it doesn't take long for them to recognize the strongest leaders and to follow them.

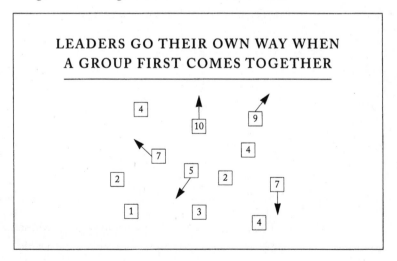

LEADERS GO THEIR OWN WAY WHEN A GROUP FIRST COMES TOGETHER

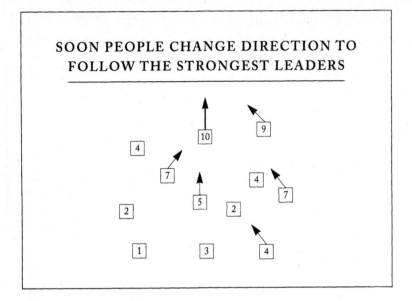

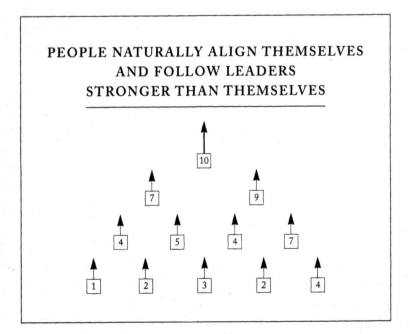

Usually the more leadership ability a person has, the more quickly he recognizes leadership—or its lack—in others. In time, people in the group get on board and follow the strongest leaders. Either that or they leave the group and pursue their own agenda.

I remember hearing a story that shows how people come to follow stronger leaders. It happened in the early 1970s when Hall of Fame basketball center Bill Walton joined Coach John Wooden's UCLA team. As a young man, Walton wore a beard. It has been said that the coach told him his players were not allowed to have facial hair. Walton, attempting to assert his independence, said that he would not shave off his beard. Wooden's no-nonsense response was, "We'll miss you, Bill." Needless to say, Walton shaved the beard.

A RESPECTED LEADER STEPS DOWN

In October of 1997, college basketball saw the retirement of another great leader, someone who engendered respect as he spent more than thirty years of his life pouring himself into others. His name is Dean Smith, and he was the head basketball coach of the University of North Carolina. He compiled a remarkable record while leading the Tar Heels and is considered one of the best to coach at any level. In thirty-two years as head coach at North Carolina, he won 879 games, more than any other coach in college basketball's history. His teams recorded 27 consecutive 20-win seasons. They won thirteen Atlantic Coast Conference titles, played in eleven Final Fours, and won two national championships.

The respect Smith has earned among his peers is tremendous. When he scheduled the press conference to announce his retirement, people such as John Thompson, head coach of

> "The leader must know, must know he knows, and must be able to make it abundantly clear to those about him that he knows."
> —Clarence B. Randall

Georgetown, whom Smith beat for the national championship in 1982, and former player Larry Brown, who now coaches the Philadelphia 76ers, came to show their support. Michael Hooker, the chancellor of the University of North Carolina, gave Smith an open invitation to do just about anything he wanted at the school in the coming years. Even the president of the United States called to honor Smith.

THOSE CLOSEST TO HIM
RESPECTED SMITH THE MOST

But the Law of Respect can be best seen in Smith's career by looking at the way his players interacted with him. They respected him for many reasons. He taught them much, about basketball as well as life. He pushed them to achieve academically, with nearly every player earning a degree. He made them winners. And he showed them incredible loyalty and respect. Charlie Scott, who played for Smith and graduated from North Carolina in 1970, advanced to play pro basketball and then went on to work as marketing director for Champion Products. Concerning his time with Smith, he said,

> As one of the first black college athletes in the ACC, I experienced many difficult moments during my time at North Carolina, but Coach Smith was always there for me. On one occasion, as we walked off the court following a game at South Carolina, one of their fans called me a "big black baboon." Two assistants had to hold Coach Smith back from going after the guy. It was the first time I had ever seen Coach Smith visibly upset, and I was shocked. But more than anything else, I was proud of him.[2]

During his time at North Carolina, Smith made quite an impact. His leadership not only won games and the respect of his players, but also helped produce a remarkable forty-nine men who went on to play professional basketball. Included in that list are greats such as Bob McAdoo, James Worthy, and of course, Michael Jordan—not only one of the best players ever to dribble a basketball, but also a fine leader in his own right.

James Jordan, Michael's father, credited Smith and his leadership for a lot of his son's success. Before a play-off game in Chicago in 1993, the elder Jordan observed:

> People underestimate the program that Dean Smith runs. He helped Michael realize his athletic ability and hone it. But more important than that, he built character in Michael that took him through his career. I don't think Michael was privileged to any more teaching than anyone else. He had the personality to go with the teaching, and at Carolina he was able to blend the two of them together. That's the only way I can look at it, and I think that's what made Michael the player he became.[3]

In recent years, Michael Jordan has been adamant about his desire to play for only one coach—Phil Jackson, the man he believes is the best in the business. It makes sense. A leader like Jordan wants to follow a strong leader. That's the Law of Respect. It's just possible that Jordan's desire got its seed when the young North Carolinian, still developing, was being led and mentored by his strong coach, Dean Smith.

HOW MANY WILL FOLLOW?

There are many ways to measure a follower's respect for his leader, but perhaps the greatest test of respect comes when a leader creates major change in an organization. I experienced this test in 1997 when I moved my company, INJOY, from San Diego, California, to

Atlanta, Georgia. I made the decision to move in early 1996 while I was on a cruise in China with my wife, Margaret. As we discussed the move and our expectations, I began weighing my influence with my core leaders. After mentally reviewing my personal history with each leader and the strength of my leadership with them, I estimated

> *The greatest test of respect comes when a leader creates major change in an organization.*

that about 50 percent of them would be willing to uproot themselves and make the move across country with me and the organization. And Margaret agreed with my assessment.

A few months later, after INJOY president Dick Peterson and I had worked through all the preliminaries of the move, I began the task of approaching my leaders individually to tell them about the decision to go to Atlanta. And one after another, the leaders told me they wanted to take the trip. I had expected about half to go. Imagine how delighted I was when I discovered that every single one of my core leaders was going with me—100 percent.

About a year has passed since we made the move, and all of those top leaders are still working with me in Atlanta. Why did so many make the trip? I know one of the reasons is that those leaders are difference makers and want to be part of the vision of our organization. Another is that I've invested a lot of time and energy in my relationships with them, adding value to their lives. But there is another, more important one. The reasons I've named wouldn't have been enough if I had been a weaker leader. Because I've spent my whole life developing my leadership skills, that has made it possible for me to lead other strong leaders. People who are 9s and 10s don't follow a 7. That's just the way leadership works. That's the secret of the Law of Respect.

THE LAW OF INTUITION

Leaders Evaluate Everything
with a Leadership Bias

D O YOU REMEMBER the old television show *Dragnet?* If you do, then you probably know the phrase that Jack Webb made famous in it: "Just the facts, ma'am, just the facts." Of all the laws of leadership, the Law of Intuition is probably the most difficult to understand. Why? Because it depends on so much more than *just the facts.* The Law of Intuition is based on facts *plus* instinct and other intangible factors. And the reality is that leadership intuition is often the factor that separates the greatest leaders from the merely good ones. Let me recount a conversation I had several years ago with a staff member named Tim Elmore. It will give you some insight into the Law of Intuition.

THE BEST LEADERS LEAD AND RESPOND

It occurred when we lived in San Diego, and three players were competing on the Chargers football team for the starting quarterback's position. Tim asked me who I thought would secure the job, and without hesitation, I said, "Stan Humphries."

"Really?" replied Tim. "I didn't think he had a chance. He's not all that big, and they say he doesn't have a strong work ethic in the weight room. He doesn't even really look like a quarterback."

"That doesn't matter," I said. "He's a better leader. Watch Stan play, and you'll see that he has the ability to read just about any situation, call the right play, and pull it off. He's the one who'll get the job." And Stan did get the job. He was so good that he was able to lead a fairly weak San Diego team to the Super Bowl in 1995.

All professional quarterbacks have physical talent. At the pro level the differences in physical ability really aren't that significant. What makes one man a third-string backup and another a Hall of Famer is intuition. The great ones can see things others can't, make changes, and move forward before others know what's happening.

IT'S INFORMED INTUITION

Several years ago I learned a lot about how quarterbacks are trained to think when I was invited to visit the University of Southern California by Coach Larry Smith. He asked me to speak to the Trojans football team before a big game. While I was there, I also visited their offensive war room. On chalkboards covering every wall, the coaches had mapped out every possible situation their team could be in—according to down, yardage, and place on the field. And for every situation, the coaches had mapped out a specific play designed to succeed, based on their years of experience and their intuitive knowledge of the game. Together those plays constituted the approach and bias they would take into the game in order to win it. The three USC quarterbacks had to memorize every one of those plays. The night before the game, I watched as the coaches fired one situ-

> *A leader has to read the situation and know instinctively what play to call.*

ation after another at those three young men, requiring them to tell which play was the right one to be called.

After they were finished, I noticed that the offensive coordinator headed for a cot in the war room, and I said, "Aren't you going home to get some sleep?"

"No," he said. "I always spend Friday night here to make sure that *I* know all the plays too."

"Yeah, but you've got all of them written down on that sheet that you'll carry with you tomorrow on the sidelines," I said. "Why don't you just use that?"

"I can't rely on that," he answered, "there isn't time. You see, by the time the ball carrier's knee touches the ground, I have to know what play to call next. There's no time to fumble around deciding what to do." It was his job to put the coaching staff's intuition into action in an instant.

LEADERSHIP IS THEIR BIAS

The kind of informed intuition that coaches and quarterbacks have on game day is similar to what leaders exhibit. Leaders see everything with a leadership bias, and as a result, they instinctively, almost automatically, know what to do. You can see this read-and-react instinct in all great leaders. For example, look at the career of U.S. Army General H. Norman Schwarzkopf. Time after time, he was assigned commands that others avoided, but he was able to turn the situations around as the result of his exceptional leadership intuition and ability to act.

> *Schwarzkopf was repeatedly able to turn bad situations around as the result of his exceptional leadership intuition.*

When Schwarzkopf had been in the army seventeen years, he finally got his chance to command a battalion. It occurred in

December 1969 during his second tour of Vietnam as a lieutenant colonel. The command, which nobody wanted, was of the First Battalion of the Sixth Infantry, called the "First of the Sixth." But because the group had such a horrible reputation, it was nicknamed the "worst of the Sixth." Confirming this was the fact that as he took command, Schwarzkopf was told that the battalion had just flunked an annual inspection. They had scored an abysmal sixteen out of one hundred points. He had only thirty days to whip his men into shape.

SEEING THROUGH A LEADERSHIP LENS

After the change-in-command ceremony, Schwarzkopf met the outgoing commander, who told him, "This is for you," handing him a bottle of Scotch. "You're gonna need it. Well, I hope you do better than I did. I tried to lead as best I could, but this is a lousy battalion. It's got lousy morale. It's got a lousy mission. Good luck to you." And with that, he left.

Schwarzkopf's intuition told him that he faced a terrible situation, but it was even worse than he had expected. His predecessor hadn't known the first thing about leadership. The man had never ventured outside the safety of the base camp to inspect his troops. And the results were appalling. The entire battalion was in chaos. The officers were indifferent, the most basic military security procedures weren't being followed, and soldiers were dying needlessly. The departing commander was right: It was a lousy battalion with lousy morale. But he didn't say that it was his fault. Based on Schwarzkopf's description, it's obvious that the previous commander had displayed no ability to read the situation, and he had failed his people as a leader.

During the next few weeks, Schwarzkopf's intuition kicked in, and he took action. He implemented military procedures, retrained the troops, developed his leaders, and gave the men direction and a sense of purpose. When it was time for the thirty-day inspection, they achieved a passing score. And the men started to think to themselves, *Hey, we can do it right. We can be a success. We're not the "worst of the Sixth" anymore.* As a result, fewer men died, morale rose, and the battalion started to become effective in its mission. Schwarzkopf's leadership was so strong and the turnaround was so effective that just a few months after he took it over, his battalion was selected to perform more difficult missions—the kind that could be carried out only by a disciplined, well-led group with strong morale.

ANOTHER LEADERSHIP CHALLENGE

Later in his career, Schwarzkopf got the opportunity to command a brigade. Once again, he accepted a post that others didn't want, and he followed someone who I believe was another poor leader. The unit was the First Reconnaissance/Commando Brigade of the Ninth Infantry at Fort Lewis, but people called it the "circus brigade" because of the way the previous commander had run it.

Schwarzkopf's leadership intuition told him that the people he commanded were good. The real problem was that their priorities were all wrong. He immediately rallied his officers, set new priorities, and empowered them to retrain their people to get back on track. As he implemented changes, his vision for them was clear in his mind. He wanted them to be ready for battle.

The unit began improving. A weaker leader might have been afraid to push the troops while they were regaining their confidence, but Schwarzkopf's intuition told him

> *People need a goal to galvanize them.*

that his people needed a goal to galvanize them. So he found one: the desert maneuvers scheduled for the following summer.

Schwarzkopf received his commander's commitment to let the

men of the First represent the division in the exercises, and then he threw himself into preparing his people to fulfill that mission. And when the maneuvers came around that summer, Schwarzkopf's three battalions went up against *thirteen* marine battalions and performed so successfully that the marine commander, a two-star general, refused to speak to Schwarzkopf when the exercises were finished.

HOW LEADERS THINK

Because of their intuition, leaders evaluate everything with a leadership bias. Some people are born with great leadership intuition. Others have to work hard to develop and hone it. But either way it evolves, the result is a combination of natural ability and learned skills. This informed intuition causes leadership issues to jump out. The best way to describe this bias is an ability to get a handle on intangible factors, understand them, and work with them to accomplish leadership goals.

Intuition helps leaders become readers of the numerous intangibles of leadership:

LEADERS ARE READERS OF THEIR SITUATION

In all kinds of circumstances, they capture details that elude others. For example, when I was the senior pastor of Skyline, my church in San Diego, there were times when I was required to travel for long periods of time. Often when I returned after being gone for ten to fourteen days, I could tell something was going on. I could feel it. And usually in an hour or so of talking with staff and getting the pulse of what was going on, I'd be able to track it down.

> *Natural ability and learned skills create an informed intuition that makes leadership issues jump out at leaders.*

LEADERS ARE READERS OF TRENDS

Everything that happens around us does so in the context of a bigger picture. Leaders have the ability to step back from what's happening at the moment and see not only where they and their people have gone, but also where they are headed in the future. It's as if they can smell change in the wind.

LEADERS ARE READERS OF THEIR RESOURCES

A major difference between achievers and leaders is the way they see resources. Successful individuals think in terms of what they can do. Successful leaders, on the other hand, see every situation in terms of available resources: money, raw materials, technology and, most important, people. They never forget that people are their greatest asset.

> *Leaders who want to succeed maximize every asset and resource they have for the benefit of their organization.*

LEADERS ARE READERS OF PEOPLE

President Lyndon Johnson once said that when you walk into a room, if you can't tell who's for you and who's against you, you don't belong in politics. That statement also applies to leadership. Intuitive leaders can sense what's happening among people and almost instantly know their hopes, fears, and concerns.

LEADERS ARE READERS OF THEMSELVES

Finally, good leaders develop the ability to read themselves—their strengths, skills, weaknesses, and current state of mind. They recognize the truth of what James Russell Lovell said: "No one can produce great things who is not thoroughly sincere in dealing with himself."

WHAT YOU SEE
RESULTS FROM WHO YOU ARE

How was Schwarzkopf able to turn around difficult assignments again and again? The answer lies in the Law of Intuition. Other officers had the benefit of the same training in soldiering and tactics. And they all had access to the same resources, so that wasn't the answer. Schwarzkopf wasn't necessarily smarter than his counterparts, either. What he brought to the table was strong leadership intuition. He saw everything with a leadership bias.

Who you are dictates what you see. If you've seen the movie *The Great Outdoors,* you may remember a scene that illustrates this idea perfectly. In the movie, John Candy plays Chet, a man vacationing with his family at a small lake community in the woods. He is unexpectedly visited by his sister-in-law and her husband, Roman (played by Dan Aykroyd), who is kind of a shady character. As the

> *Who you are dictates what you see.*

two men sit on the porch of their cabin overlooking the lake and miles of beautiful forest, they start to talk. And Roman, who sees himself as a wheeler-dealer, shares his vision with Chet: "I'll tell you what I see when I look out there . . . I see the underdeveloped resources of northern Minnesota, Wisconsin, and Michigan. I see a syndicated development consortium exploiting over a billion and a half dollars in forest products. I see a paper mill and—if the strategic metals are there—a mining operation; a green belt between the condos on the lake and a waste management facility . . . Now I ask you, what do you see?"

"I, uh, I just see trees," answers Chet.

"Well," says Roman, "nobody ever accused you of having a grand vision."

Chet saw trees because he was there to enjoy the scenery. Roman saw opportunity because he was a businessman whose desire was to make money. How you see the world around you is determined by who you are.

THREE LEVELS OF LEADERSHIP INTUITION

Just about everyone is capable of developing a degree of leadership intuition, though we don't all start off at the same place. I've found that all people fit into three major intuition levels:

1. THOSE WHO NATURALLY SEE IT

Some people are born with exceptional leadership gifts. They instinctively understand people and know how to move them from point A to point B. Even when they're kids, they act as leaders. Watch them on the playground, and you can see everyone is following them. People with natural leadership intuition can build upon it and become world-class leaders of the highest caliber. This natural ability is often the difference between a 9 (an excellent leader) and a 10 (a world-class leader).

2. THOSE WHO ARE NURTURED TO SEE IT

Not everyone starts off with great instincts, but whatever abilities people have can be nurtured and developed. The ability to think like a leader is *informed* intuition. Even someone who doesn't start off as a natural leader can become an excellent one. People who don't develop their intuition are condemned to be blindsided in their leadership for the rest of their lives.

3. THOSE WHO WILL NEVER SEE IT

I believe nearly everyone is capable of developing leadership skills and intuition. But occasionally, I run across someone who doesn't seem to have a leadership bone in his body *and* who has no interest in developing the skills necessary to lead. Those people will never think like anything but followers.

LEADERS SOLVE PROBLEMS
USING THE LAW OF INTUITION

Whenever leaders find themselves facing a problem, they automatically measure it—and begin solving it—using the Law of Intuition. They evaluate everything with a leadership bias. For example, you can see where leadership intuition came into play recently at Apple Computer. Just about everybody knows the success story of Apple. The company was created in 1976 by Steve Jobs and Steve Wozniak in Jobs's father's garage. Just four years later, the business went public, opening at twenty-two dollars a share and selling 4.6 million shares. It made more than forty employees and investors millionaires overnight.

> *Whenever leaders find themselves facing a problem, they automatically measure it—and begin solving it—using the Law of Intuition.*

But Apple's story isn't all positive. Since those early years, Apple's success, stock value, and ability to capture customers have fluctuated wildly. Jobs left Apple in 1985, having been pushed out in a battle with CEO John Sculley, the former Pepsi president whom Jobs had recruited in 1983. Sculley was followed by Michael Spindler in 1993 and then Gilbert Amelio in 1996. None of them was able to reestablish Apple's previous success. In its glory days, Apple had sold 14.6 percent of all personal computers in the United States. By 1997, sales were depressed to 3.5 percent. That was when Apple again looked to the leadership of its original founder, Steve Jobs, for help. The failing company believed he could save it.

REINVENTING APPLE

Jobs intuitively reviewed the situation and immediately took action. He knew that improvement was impossible without a change in leadership, so he quickly dismissed all but two of the previous board members and installed new ones. Executive leadership also experienced positive change at his hands.

Once new leaders were in place, he looked at the company's focus. Jobs wanted to get back to the basics of what Apple had always done best: use its individuality to create products that made a difference. Jobs said, "We've reviewed the road map of new products and axed more than 70% of the projects, keeping the 30% that were gems. Plus we're adding new ones that are a whole new paradigm of looking at computers." He also sensed a problem with the company's marketing, so he fired the ad agency and held a competition for the account among three firms.[1]

None of those actions was especially surprising. But Jobs also did something that really showed the Law of Intuition in action.

> *Improvement is impossible without a change in leadership.*

He made a leadership decision that went absolutely against the grain of Apple's previous thinking. It was an incredible intuitive leadership leap. Jobs created a strategic alliance with the man whom Apple employees considered to be their archenemy—Bill Gates. Jobs explained, "I called Bill and said Microsoft and Apple should work more closely together, but we have this issue to resolve, this intellectual-property dispute. Let's resolve it."

They negotiated a deal quickly, which settled Apple's lawsuit against Microsoft. Gates promised to pay off Apple and invest $150 million in nonvoting stock. That cleared the way for future partnership and brought much-needed capital to the company. It was something only an intuitive leader would have done. Not surprisingly, when Jobs announced the new alliance to a meeting of the Apple faithful, they booed. But on Wall Street, Apple stock value immediately soared 33 percent to $26.31.[2]

Apple looks as if it's turning around. Prior to Jobs's return, the company had posted net quarterly losses the previous year totaling more than $1 billion. However, in the first fiscal quarter of 1998, Apple finally recorded a net profit of $47 million. In the long run, it's hard to know whether the company will ever recapture its former success. But at least it now has a fighting chance.

> *Leadership is more art than science.*

Leadership is really more art than science. The principles of leadership are constant, but the application changes with every leader and every situation. That's why it requires intuition. Without it, you can get blindsided, and that's one of the worst things that can happen to a leader. If you want to lead long, you've got to obey the Law of Intuition.

THE LAW OF MAGNETISM

Who You Are Is Who You Attract

E FFECTIVE LEADERS ARE always on the lookout for good people. I think each of us carries around a mental list of what kind of people we would like to have in our organization. Think about it. Do you know who you're looking for right now? What is your profile of perfect employees? What qualities do these people possess? Do you want them to be aggressive and entrepreneurial? Are you looking for leaders? Do you care whether they are in their twenties, forties, or sixties? Stop right now, take a moment, and make a list of the qualities you'd like to see in the people on your team. Find a pencil or pen, and do it now before you read any farther.

MY PEOPLE WOULD HAVE THESE QUALITIES

_____   _____

_____   _____

_____   _____

_____   _____

_____

_____   _____
_____   _____
_____   _____
_____

Now, what will determine whether the people you want are the people you get, whether they will possess the qualities you desire? You may be surprised by the answer. Believe it or not, who you get is not determined by what you *want*. It's determined by who you *are*. Go back to the list you just made, and next to each characteristic you identified, check to see if you possess that quality. For example, if you

> *Who you get is not determined by what you want. It's determined by who you are.*

wrote that you would like "great leaders" and you are an excellent leader, that's a match. Put a check by it. But if your leadership is no better than average, put an X and write "only average leader" next to it. If you wrote that you want people who are "entrepreneurial" and you possess that quality, put a check.

Otherwise, mark it with an X, and so on. Now review the whole list.

If you see a whole bunch of Xs, then you're in trouble because the people you describe are not the type who will want to follow you. In most situations, you draw people to you who possess the same qualities you do. That's the Law of Magnetism: Who you are is who you attract.

FROM MUSICIANSHIP TO LEADERSHIP

When I was a kid, my mother used to tell me that birds of a feather flock together. I thought that was a wise saying when I was spending time with my older brother, Larry, and playing ball. He was a good athlete, so I figured that made me one too. As I grew up, I think I instinctively recognized that good students spent time with good students, people who only wanted to play stuck together, and so on. But I don't think I *really* understood the impact of the Law of Magnetism until I moved to San Diego, California, and became the leader of my last church.

My predecessor at Skyline Church was Dr. Orval Butcher. He is a wonderful man with many fine qualities. One of his best is his musicianship. He plays piano and has a beautiful Irish tenor voice, even today in his eighties. At the time I arrived in 1981, Skyline had a solid reputation for fine music. It was nationally known for its outstanding musical productions. In fact, the church was filled with talented musicians and vocalists. And in the twenty-seven years Dr. Butcher led the church, only two music directors worked for him— an unbelievable track record. (In comparison, during my fourteen years there, I employed five people in that capacity.)

Why were there so many exceptional musicians at Skyline? The answer lies in the Law of Magnetism. People with musical talent were naturally attracted to Dr. Butcher. They respected him and understood him. They shared his motivation and values. They were on the same page with him. In contrast, I *enjoy* music, but I am not a musician. It's funny, but when I interviewed for the position at Skyline, one of the first questions they asked me was whether I could sing. They were very disappointed when I told them no.

After I came on board at the church, the number of new musicians declined quickly. We still had more than our share, because Dr. Butcher had created momentum and a wonderful legacy in that area. But do you know what kind of people started coming instead? Leaders. By the time I left Skyline, not only was the church filled with hundreds of excellent leaders, but the church had also equipped and sent out hundreds of men and women as leaders during the time I was there. The reason was the Law of Magnetism. Our organization became a magnet for people with leadership ability.

PEOPLE LIKE YOU WILL SEEK YOU OUT

Of course, it is possible for a leader to go out and recruit people unlike himself. Good leaders know that one secret to success is to staff their weaknesses. That way they can focus and function in their areas of strength while others take care of the important matters that would otherwise be neglected. But it's crucial to recognize that people who are different will not naturally be attracted to you. Leaders draw people who are like themselves.

> *It is possible for a leader to go out and recruit people unlike himself, but those are not the people he will naturally attract.*

For example, think about the NFL's Dallas Cowboys. In the sixties and seventies, the Cowboys' image was squeaky clean. Tex Schramm was the president and general manager of the team, and Tom Landry was the coach. Players were men like Roger Staubach, called "Captain Comeback," a family man with strong values similar to those of Tom Landry. In those days, the Cowboys were called "America's team." They were one of the most popular groups of athletes around the country. And they were respected not only because of the talent and character of the individuals associated with the organization, but also because of their incredible ability to work together as a team. As they developed a winning tradition in Dallas, they continued to attract more winners.

But for the past ten years, the Dallas Cowboys have been a very different kind of team. They have changed, and their image has too. Instead of working together as a team, they sometimes appear to be a loosely associated group of individuals who are in the game solely for their own benefit. (Unfortunately, because the country has also changed, they could still be called "America's team.") Various players, such as wide receiver Michael Irvin, have been on the wrong side of the law. Even Coach Barry Switzer found himself in trouble several times, such as when he tried to take a loaded gun through the security gate at an airport. Why has the complexion of the team changed so drastically? It's the Law of Magnetism. In 1989 the Cowboys' ownership changed. The new owner, Jerry Jones, is an individualist and something of a maverick. He had no qualms about going out and signing his own deals with shoe and soft drink companies despite the fact that all the NFL teams had already signed a collective endorsement contract with a competitor.

It's little wonder that the Cowboys don't enjoy the reputation they once had, even with their recent Super Bowl victories. Al McGuire, former head basketball coach of Marquette University, once said, "A team should be an extension of the coach's personality. My teams were arrogant and obnoxious." I say that teams cannot be anything *but* an extension of the coach's personality. Fortunately, Dallas just brought on board a new coach, Chan Gailey. He is a good leader with strong character and values. If he is given enough time and authority, he may be able to attract enough additional people like himself to turn the Cowboys around. Then the Law of Magnetism will be able to work *for* Dallas, but it won't happen overnight.

WHERE DO THEY MATCH UP?

Maybe you've started thinking about the people that you have attracted in your organization. You might say to yourself, "Wait a minute. I can name twenty things that make my people different from me." And my response would be, "Of course, you can." But the people who are drawn to you probably have more similarities than differences, especially in a few key areas. Take a look at the following characteristics. You will probably find

> *If you think your people are negative, then you better check your attitude.*

that you and the people who follow you share common ground in several of these key areas:

ATTITUDE

Rarely have I seen positive and negative people attracted to one another. People who view life as a series of opportunities and exciting challenges don't want to hear others talk about how bad things are all the time. I know that's true for me. I can't think of a single negative person in my organizations. And if you were to talk to my four company presidents and all my top managers, you'd find that every one of them is an especially positive person.

GENERATION

People tend to attract others of roughly the same age. My top leaders are a good example. Three of my four company presidents are only one or two years different in age from me. And that same pattern can be seen in other areas of my companies, such as among some managers at INJOY. For instance, Kevin Small, who heads the seminar marketing area, is a sharp, aggressive young man in his twenties. Can you guess what kind of people are attracted to him? Most of them are sharp and aggressive and in their twenties. Who you are is who you attract.

BACKGROUND

In the chapter on the Law of Process, I wrote about Theodore Roosevelt. One of his memorable accomplishments is his daring charge up San Juan Hill with the Rough Riders during the Spanish-American War. Roosevelt personally recruited that all-volunteer cavalry company, and it was said to be a remarkably peculiar group of people. It was comprised primarily of two types of men: wealthy aristocrats from the Northeast and cowboys from the Wild West. Why? Because TR was an aristocratic-born, Harvard-educated New Yorker who turned himself into a real-life cowboy and big-game hunter in the Dakotas of the West. He was a strong and genuine leader in both worlds, and as a result, he attracted both kinds of people.

VALUES

People are attracted to leaders whose values are similar to their own. Think about the people who flocked to President John F. Kennedy after he was elected in 1960. He was a young idealist who wanted to change the world, and he attracted people with a similar profile. When he formed the Peace Corps and called people to service, saying, "Ask not what your country can do for you; ask what you can do for your country," thousands of young, idealistic people stepped forward to answer the challenge.

It doesn't matter whether the shared values are positive or negative. Either way, the attraction is equally strong. Think about someone like Adolf Hitler. He was a very strong leader (as you can judge by his level of influence). But his values were rotten to the core. What kinds of people did he attract? Leaders with similar values: Hermann Goering, founder of the Gestapo; Joseph Goebbels, a bitter anti-Semite who ran Hitler's propaganda machine; Reinhard Heydrich, second in command of the Nazi secret police, who ordered mass executions of Nazi opponents; and Heinrich Himmler, chief of the SS and director of the Gestapo who initiated the systematic execution of Jews. They were all strong leaders, and they were all utterly evil men. The Law of Magnetism is powerful. Whatever character you possess you will likely find in the people who follow you.

LIFE EXPERIENCE

Life experience is another area of attraction for people. For example, anytime I speak to a new audience, I can tell within thirty seconds what kind of speaker they are used to hearing. If they regularly listen to gifted and energetic communicators, they are a sharp and responsive audience. You can see it in their faces. Their sense of expectation is high, their body language is positive, and when you get ready to speak, they have paper and pencil ready to take notes. But if people are used to a poor communicator, I find that they just check out mentally.

LEADERSHIP ABILITY

Finally, the people you attract will have leadership ability similar to your own. As I said in discussing the Law of Respect, people naturally follow leaders stronger than themselves. But you also have to factor in the Law of Magnetism, which states that who you are is who you attract. What that means is that if you are a 7 when it comes to leadership, you are more likely to draw 5s and 6s to you than 2s and 3s. The leaders you attract will be similar in style and ability to you.

HISTORY CHANGES COURSE

A vivid example of the Law of Magnetism can be seen among the military leaders of the Civil War. When the Southern states seceded, there were questions about which side many of the generals would fight for. Robert E. Lee was considered the best general in the nation, and President Lincoln actually offered him command of the Union army. But Lee would never consider fighting against his native Virginia. He declined the offer and joined the Confederacy—and the best generals in the land followed him.

> *The better leader you are, the better leaders you will attract.*

If Lee had chosen to lead an army for the Union instead, many other good generals would have followed him north. As a result, the war probably would have been much shorter. It might have lasted two years instead of five—and hundreds of thousands of lives would have been saved. It just goes to show you that the better leader you are, the better leaders you will attract. And that has an incredible impact on everything you do.

How do the people you are currently attracting to your organization or department look to you? Are they the strong, capable potential leaders you desire? Or could they be better? Remember, their quality does not ultimately depend on a hiring process, a human resources department, or even what you consider to be the quality of your area's applicant pool. It depends on you. Who you are is who you attract. That is the Law of Magnetism.

> *If you think the people you attract could be better, then it's time for you to improve yourself.*

THE LAW OF CONNECTION

Leaders Touch a Heart Before
They Ask for a Hand

I LOVE COMMUNICATING. It's one of the joys of my life and one of my passions. Although I've spent more than thirty years speaking professionally, I'm always looking for ways to grow and keep improving in that area. That's why I try to see first-rate communicators in person when I get the chance. For instance, I made a trip to San Jose, California, to see an event sponsored by the local chamber of commerce. Speaking that day was an all-star cast of communicators: Mark Russell, who used humor so effectively; Mario Cuomo, who infused passion into everything he said; the brilliant Malcolm Forbes, whose insight made every subject he talked about seem brand new; and Colin Powell, whose confidence gave everyone in the audience security and hope. Every one of those communicators was strong and was able to develop an incredible rapport with the audience. But as good as they were, none was as good as my favorite. Head and shoulders above the rest stood Elizabeth Dole.

THE AUDIENCE'S BEST FRIEND

No doubt you've heard of Elizabeth Dole. She is a lawyer by trade, was a cabinet member in the Reagan and Bush administrations, and is now the president of the American Red Cross. She is a marvelous communicator. Her particular gift, which she demonstrated in San Jose that day, was making me and everyone else in her audience feel as though she was really our friend. She made me glad I was there. The bottom line is that she really knows how to connect with people.

In 1996, she demonstrated that ability to the whole country when she spoke at the Republican National Convention. If you watched it on television, you know what I'm talking about. When Elizabeth Dole walked out into the audience that night, they felt that she was their best friend. She was able to develop an amazing connection with them. I also felt that connection, even though I was sitting in my living room at home watching her on television. Once she finished her talk, I would have followed her anywhere.

BOB NEVER MADE THE CONNECTION

Also speaking at that convention was Bob Dole, Elizabeth's husband—not surprising since he was the Republican nominee for the presidential race. Anyone who watched would have observed a remarkable difference between the communication abilities of the two speakers. Where Elizabeth was warm and approachable, Bob appeared stern and distant. Throughout the campaign, he never seemed to be able to connect with the people.

Many factors come into play in the election of a president of the United States, but not least among them is the ability of a candidate to connect with his audience. A lot has been written about the Kennedy-Nixon debates of the 1960 election. One of the reasons Kennedy succeeded was that he was able to make the television audience feel connected to him. The same kind of connection developed between Ronald Reagan and his audiences. And in the 1992 election, Bill Clinton worked extremely hard to develop a sense of connection with the American people—to do it he even appeared on the talk show *Arsenio* and played the saxophone.

I believe Bob Dole is a good man. But I also know he never connected with the people. Ironically, after the presidential race was over, he appeared on *Saturday Night Live,* a show that made fun of him during the entire campaign, implying that he was humorless and out of touch. On the show Dole came across as relaxed, approachable, and able to make fun of himself. And he was a hit with the audience. I can't help wondering what might have happened if he had done more of that early in the campaign.

THE HEART COMES FIRST

Effective leaders know that you first have to touch people's hearts before you ask them for a hand. That is the Law of Connection. All great communicators recognize this truth and act on it almost instinctively. You can't move people to action unless you first move them with emotion. The heart comes before the head.

> *You can't move people to action unless you first move them with emotion. The heart comes before the head.*

An outstanding orator and African-American leader of the nineteenth century was Frederick Douglass. It's said that he had a remarkable ability to connect with people and move their hearts when he spoke. Historian Lerone Bennett said of Douglass, "He could make people *laugh* at a slave owner preaching the duties of Christian obedience; could make them *see* the humiliation of a Black maiden ravished by a brutal slave owner; could make them *hear* the sobs of a mother separated from her child. Through him, people could cry, curse, and *feel;* through him they could *live* slavery."

PUBLIC AND PRIVATE CONNECTION

Connecting with people isn't something that needs to happen only when a leader is communicating to groups of people. It needs to happen with individuals. The stronger the relationship and connection between individuals, the more likely the follower will want to help the leader. That is one of the most important principles I've taught my staff over the years. My staff at Skyline used to groan every time I would say, "People don't care how much you know until they know

> *The stronger the relationship and connection between individuals, the more likely the follower will want to help the leader.*

how much you care," but they also knew that it was true. You develop credibility with people when you connect with them and show that you genuinely want to help them.

The greatest leaders are able to connect on both levels: with individuals and with an audience. A perfect example was Ronald Reagan. His ability to develop rapport with an audience is reflected in the nickname he received as president: the Great Communi-

cator. But he also had the ability to touch the hearts of the individuals close to him. Former Reagan speechwriter Peggy Noonan said that when the president used to return to the White House from long trips and the staff heard his helicopter landing on the lawn, everyone would stop working, and staff member Donna Elliott would say, "Daddy's home!" It was an indication of the affection his people felt for him.

You don't need the charisma of Ronald Reagan to connect with people. You will sometimes discover the ability to connect with people where you would least expect to find it. I was reminded of that recently as I read about the funeral of Sonny Bono. Though he had succeeded in recent years in the world of politics, having served as the mayor of Palm Springs and a member of the U.S. House of Representatives, most people remember Bono from his show business days. He was hard to take seriously. He wore outrageous clothes. He was always the butt of then wife Cher's jokes, and he couldn't sing. But the man knew how to connect with others. At his funeral, House Speaker Newt Gingrich said of Bono:

> You looked at him and thought to yourself: "This can't be a famous person." He smiled, he said something, then you thought to yourself: "This can't be a serious person." Four jokes and two stories later you were pouring your heart out to him, he was helping you solve a problem and you began to realize this is a very hard-working, very thoughtful man who covered up a great deal of his abilities with his wonderful sense of humor and his desire to make you bigger than him so he could serve you, which would then make it easier for you to do something the two of you needed to do together.[1]

Bono understood the Law of Connection. He won people over before he enlisted their help. He knew that you have to touch a heart before you ask for a hand.

CONNECT WITH PEOPLE ONE AT A TIME

A key to connecting with others is recognizing that even in a group, you have to relate to people as individuals. General Norman Schwarzkopf remarked, "I have seen competent leaders who stood in front of a platoon and all they saw was a platoon. But great leaders stand in front of a platoon and see it as 44 individuals, each of whom has aspirations, each of whom wants to live, each of whom wants to do good."[2]

> *To connect with people in a group, relate to them as individuals.*

I've had the opportunity to speak to some wonderful audiences during the course of my career. The largest have been in stadiums where 60,000 to 70,000 people were in attendance. Some of my colleagues who also speak for a living have asked me, "How in the world do you speak to that many people?" The secret is simple. I don't try to talk to the thousands. I focus on talking to one person. That's the only way to connect with people.

IT'S THE LEADER'S JOB

Some leaders have problems with the Law of Connection because they believe that connecting is the responsibility of followers. That is especially true of positional leaders. They often think, *I'm the boss. I have the position. These are my employees. Let them come to me.* But successful leaders who obey the Law of Connection are always initiators. They take the first step with others and then make the effort to continue building relationships. That's not always easy, but it's important to the success of the organization. A leader has to do it, no matter how many obstacles there might be.

I learned this lesson in 1972 when I was faced with a very difficult situation. I was moving to Lancaster, Ohio, where I would be taking over the leadership of a church. Before I accepted the position, I found out from a friend that the church had just gone through a big battle related to a building project. Heading up one of the factions was the number one influencer in the church, a man named Jim Butz who was the elected lay leader of the congregation. And I also heard that Jim had a reputation for being negative and something of a maverick. He liked to use his influence to move the people in directions that didn't always help the organization.

Because the previous senior pastor had butted heads with Jim more than a few times, I knew my best chance for being successful in leadership there was to make a connection with Jim. So the first thing I did when I got there was to make an appointment to meet him in my office.

Jim was a big man. He was about six feet four inches tall and weighed about 250 pounds—the kind of guy who could go bear hunting with nothing but a switch. He was very intimidating, and he was about sixty-five years old. I, on the other hand, was only twenty-five. When he came in, I said, "Jim, I know you're the influencer in this church, and I want you to know that I've decided I'm going to do everything in my power to build a good relationship with you. I'd like to meet with you every Tuesday for lunch at the Holiday Inn to talk through issues. While I'm the leader here, I'll never take any decision to the people without first discussing it with you. I really want to work with you.

> *It's the leader's job to initiate connection with the people.*

"But I also want you to know that I've heard you're a very negative person," I said, "and that you like to fight battles. If you decide to work against me, I'll guess we'll just have to be on opposite sides. And because you have so much influence, I know you'll win most of the time in the beginning. But I'm going to develop relationships with people and draw new people to this church, and someday, I'll have greater influence than you.

"But I don't want to battle you," I continued. "You're sixty-five years old right now. Let's say you've got another ten to fifteen years of good health and productivity ahead of you. If you want, you can make these years your very best and make your life count. We can do a lot of great things together at this church, but the decision is yours."

When I finished, Jim didn't say a word. He got up from his seat, walked into the hall, and stopped to take a drink at the water fountain. I followed him out and waited. After a long time, he stood up straight and turned around. When he did, I could see that tears were rolling down his cheeks. And then he gave me a great big bear hug and said, "You can count on me to be on your side."

And Jim did get on my side. As it turned out, he did live about another ten years, and because he was willing to help me, we accomplished some positive things together at that church. But it never would have happened if I hadn't had the courage to try to make a connection with him that first day in my office.

THE TOUGHER THE CHALLENGE, THE GREATER THE CONNECTION

Never underestimate the power of building relationships with people before asking them to follow you. If you've ever studied the lives of notable military commanders, you have probably noticed that the best ones practiced the Law of Connection. I once read that during World War I in France, General Douglas MacArthur told a battalion commander before a daring charge, "Major, when the signal comes to go over the top, I want you to go first, before your men. If you do, they'll follow." Then MacArthur removed the Distinguished Service Cross from his uniform and pinned it on the major. He had, in effect, awarded him for heroism before asking him to exhibit it. And of course, the major led his men, they followed him over the top, and they achieved their objective.

Not all military examples of the Law of Connection are quite so dramatic. For example, it's said that Napoleon made it a practice to know every one of his officers by name and to remember where they lived and which battles they had fought with him. Robert E. Lee was known to visit the men in their campsites the night before any major battle. Often he met the next day's challenges without having slept. More recently, I read about how Norman Schwarzkopf often found ways of connecting with his troops. On Christmas in 1990 during the

Persian Gulf War, he spent the day among the men and women who were so far away from their families. In his autobiography, he says,

> I started at Lockheed Village . . . Some [troops] had already sat down to dinner, though it was only noon, because they were eating in shifts. I shook a lot of hands. Next I went back out to the Escan Village, where there were three huge mess halls in tents. At the first a long line of troops stretched out the entryway. I shook hands with everyone in the line, went behind the serving counter to greet the cooks and helpers, and worked my way through the mess hall, hitting every table, wishing everyone Merry Christmas. Then I went into the second and third dining facilities and did the same thing. I came back to the first mess tent and repeated the exercise, because by this time there was an entirely new set of faces. Then I sat down with some of the troops and had my dinner. In the course of four hours, I must have shaken four thousand hands.[3]

> *It may sound corny, but it's really true: People don't care how much you know until they know how much you care.*

Schwarzkopf didn't have to do that, but he did. He used one of the most effective methods for connecting with others, something I call walking slowly through the crowd. It may sound corny, but it's really true: People don't care how much you know until they know how much you care.

THE RESULT OF CONNECTION

When a leader has done the work to connect with his people, you can see it in the way the organization functions. Among employees there are incredible loyalty and a strong work ethic. The vision of the leader becomes the aspiration of the people. The impact is incredible.

You can also see the results in other ways. On Boss's Day in 1994, a full-page ad appeared in *USA Today*. It was contracted and paid for by the employees of Southwest Airlines, and it was addressed to Herb Kelleher, the company's CEO:

Thanks, Herb
For remembering every one of our names.
For supporting the Ronald McDonald House.
For helping load baggage on Thanksgiving.
For giving everyone a kiss (and we mean everyone).
For listening.
For running the only profitable major airline.
For singing at our holiday party.
For singing only once a year.
For letting us wear shorts and sneakers to work.
For golfing at The LUV Classic with only one club.
For outtalking Sam Donaldson.
For riding your Harley Davidson into Southwest Headquarters.
For being a friend, not just a boss.
Happy Boss's Day from Each One of Your 16,000 Employees[4]

A display of affection like that occurs only when a leader has worked hard to connect with his people.

Don't ever underestimate the importance of building relational bridges between yourself and the people you lead. There's an old saying: To lead yourself, use your head; to lead others, use your heart. That's the nature of the Law of Connection. Always touch a person's heart before you ask him for a hand.

> *To lead yourself, use your head; to lead others, use your heart.*

11

THE LAW OF THE INNER CIRCLE

*A Leader's Potential Is Determined
by Those Closest to Him*

IN 1981, I RECEIVED a marvelous offer. I was working as an executive director at Wesleyan World Headquarters when I was given the opportunity to become the leader of the largest church in the Wesleyan denomination. The name of the church was Skyline, and it was located in the San Diego, California, area.

The church had a great history. It had been founded in the 1950s by a wonderful man named Orval Butcher, and he was retiring after serving there for twenty-seven years. Dr. Butcher had touched the lives of thousands of people with his leadership, and the church had a strong, nationally recognized reputation. It was a good church, but it did have one problem. It had not grown in years. After making it to a little more than one thousand members, it had reached a plateau.

The first time I flew out to talk with the board, I knew that Skyline was the place I was supposed to be. I immediately called and told my wife, Margaret, that we should start packing and preparing for a move. And as soon as they offered me the job, off we went with our two kids to San Diego.

THE 21 IRREFUTABLE LAWS OF LEADERSHIP

> *Every leader's potential is determined by the people closest to him. No matter what I did with that staff, they would never be able to take the organization to the place we needed to go.*

As we drove across the country, I began thinking about the task ahead. I was really looking forward to the challenge of taking Skyline to a new level. After we arrived, I met with each of the staff members to assess individual abilities. Almost immediately I discovered why the church had flat-lined. The staff were good people, but they weren't strong leaders. No matter what I did with them, they would never be able to take the organization to the place we needed to go. You see, every leader's potential is determined by the people closest to him. If those people are strong, then the leader can make a huge impact. If they are weak, he can't. That is the Law of the Inner Circle.

THREE PHASES TO NEW GROWTH

The task that lay ahead of me was clear. I needed to remove the weak leaders I possessed and bring in better ones. That was the only way I would be able to turn the situation around. Mentally, I divided the people into three groups according to their ability to lead and deliver results. The first group I wanted to deal with was the bottom third, the staff contributing least to the organization. I knew I could dismiss them right away because the impact of their departure could be nothing but positive. I immediately replaced them with the best people I could find.

I then began working on the middle third. One by one, as I found good leaders from outside the organization, I brought them in and let go the weakest of the existing staff. It took me another year to process out the old middle group. By the end of three years, I had completely cleaned house, leaving only two on staff out of the original group. And because the inner circle had gone to a new level, the organization was able to go to a new level. On the new staff, even the weakest of the new people were stronger than all the old ones I had let go.

The staff continued to grow in strength. I developed the people to make them better leaders. And anytime a staff member left, I searched for someone even better as a replacement. As a result, the impact on Skyline was incredible. Almost as soon as I made the initial staff changes in 1981, we started growing again. In fewer than ten years, the church became three times the size it had been when I started. And the annual budget, which was $800,000 when I arrived, grew to more than $5 million a year.

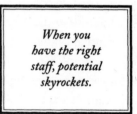

When you have the right staff, potential skyrockets.

The growth and success we experienced at Skyline were due to the Law of the Inner Circle. When we had the right staff, our potential skyrocketed. And in 1995 when I left, other leaders from

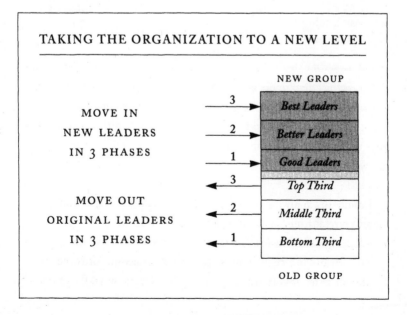

TAKING THE ORGANIZATION TO A NEW LEVEL

NEW GROUP

MOVE IN NEW LEADERS IN 3 PHASES	3 →	*Best Leaders*
	2 →	*Better Leaders*
	1 →	*Good Leaders*
MOVE OUT ORIGINAL LEADERS IN 3 PHASES	← 3	*Top Third*
	← 2	*Middle Third*
	← 1	*Bottom Third*

OLD GROUP

around the country sought to hire my key staff members for their own organizations. They recognized the power of the Law of the Inner Circle and wanted to hire the very best they could find to boost their potential.

EVERY ORGANIZATION HAS AN INNER CIRCLE

Look at an organization in just about any profession and you can see the Law of the Inner Circle at work. For example, in 1997 baseball's Florida Marlins assembled an awesome group of players together as a team. What was the result? They won the World Series. But once their championship season was over, they began dismantling the team. It was a "fire sale" similar to the one that the San Diego Padres

> There are no Lone Ranger leaders. Think about it: If you're alone, you're not leading anybody, are you?

management held in the early 1990s before their team was sold. The result in Florida will be the same as it was in San Diego. Without their key players, their inner circle, the Marlins will fall into the ranks of the mediocre. The potential of the leader—along with the potential of the whole organization—is determined by those closest to him.

Knowing what I do about the impact of the Law of the Inner Circle, I am amazed when I meet people who continue to hold up the Lone Ranger as their model for leadership. One of the best illustrations of how unrealistic that ideal of leadership really is can be found in *American Spirit* by Lawrence Miller:

Problems are always solved in the same way. The Lone Ranger and his faithful Indian companion . . . come riding into town. The Lone Ranger, with his mask and mysterious identity, background, and life-style, never becomes intimate with those whom he will help. His power is partly in his mystique. Within ten

minutes the Lone Ranger has understood the problem, identified who the bad guys are, and has set out to catch them. He
quickly outwits the bad guys, draws his gun, and has them
behind bars. And then there was always that wonderful scene at
the end [where] the helpless victims are standing in front of their
ranch or in the town square marveling at how wonderful it is
now that they have been saved.[1]

That's baloney. There are no Lone Ranger leaders. Think about it: If
you're alone, you're not *leading* anybody, are you?

Leadership expert Warren Bennis was right when he maintained,
"The leader finds greatness in the group, and he or she helps the
members find it in themselves."[2] Think of any highly effective leader,
and you will find someone who surrounded himself with a strong
inner circle. My friend Joseph Fisher reminded me of that as he
talked about the impact of evangelist Billy Graham. His success has
come as the result of a fantastic inner circle: Ruth Bell Graham,
Grady Wilson, Cliff Barrows, and George Beverly Shea. They made
him better than he ever would have been alone. You could say the
same thing of two-term President Ronald Reagan. He was successful because he surrounded himself with good people.

THE BEST DON'T ALWAYS DO THE BEST

At a conference where I was teaching the Law of the Inner Circle, a
man named Ashley Randall of Woodbine, Georgia, came up to me
during a break and said, "John, you're right about the power of asso-
ciation with good people. I bicycle a lot, and I follow the world-class
racers. In endurance bicycle races like the Tour de France, the winner
is almost always the person who is racing with the strongest team.
They aren't the first to finish every day, but they are always in the first
pack to finish each day.

"I've also found that to be true myself," he said. "I've competed in a couple of triathlons, and I can testify that I swim, bike, and run better on the day of the race than I do any other day of training. It's because I am surrounded by people who are swimming, biking, and running at a higher level and doing it with me."

You can tell when a leader has mastered the Law of the Inner Circle. For example, Jack Welch, chairman and CEO of General Electric, doesn't leave to chance the formation of the top inner circles within his organization. Since assuming leadership of GE in 1981, he has personally given his okay to every general manager's circle of executives—that's five hundred positions in all.

THE VALUE OF RAISING UP THE RIGHT PEOPLE IN YOUR INNER CIRCLE

Under the best circumstances, a leader should try to raise up people for his inner circle from within his organization. Of course, that's not always possible, as my story from Skyline shows. But you can't beat the satisfaction and rewards of bringing up men and women from the "farm team."

Hewlett-Packard manager Ned Barnholt believes there are three groups of people in an organization when it comes to their response to leadership and its impact: (1) those who get it almost immediately and they're off and running with it; (2) those who are skeptical and not sure what to do with it; and (3) another third who start out negative and hope it will go away. "I used to spend most of my time with those who were the most negative," says Barnholt, "trying to convince them to change. Now I spend my time with the people in the first [group]. I'm investing in my best assets"[3] That attitude pays rich dividends in the future.

You may be wondering where you should be spending your time in your organization. You should try to bring five types of people into your inner circle. All of them can add tremendous value to you and your organization.

I. POTENTIAL VALUE—THOSE WHO RAISE UP THEMSELVES

The first ability that every leader must have is the ability to lead and motivate himself. Always keep your eyes open for people with potential.

2. POSITIVE VALUE—THOSE WHO RAISE MORALE IN THE ORGANIZATION

Here is an old poem by Ella Wheeler Wilcox that my mother used to recite to me:

> There are two kinds of people on earth today,
> Just two kinds of people, no more, I say.
> Not the good and the bad, for 'tis well understood
> That the good are half-bad and the bad are half-good.
> No! The two kinds of people on earth I mean
> Are the people who lift and the people who lean.

People who are able to lift up others and boost the morale in an organization are invaluable, and they are always a tremendous asset to a leader's inner circle.

3. PERSONAL VALUE—THOSE WHO RAISE UP THE LEADER

A friend once told me, "It's lonely at the top, so you had better know why you're there." It's true that leaders carry a heavy load. When you're out front, you can be an easy target. But you don't have to go it alone. That's why I say, "It's lonely at the top, so you'd better take someone with you." Who could be better than

> *It's lonely at the top, so you'd better take someone with you.*

someone who lifts you up, not as a yes-man, but as a solid supporter and friend? Solomon of ancient Israel recognized this truth: "As iron sharpens iron, friends sharpen the minds of each other."[4] Seek for your inner circle people who help you improve.

4. PRODUCTION VALUE—THOSE WHO RAISE UP OTHERS

Radio comedian Fred Allen said about television host Ed Sullivan, "He'll be around as long as other people have talent." Though he said it as a joke, there was a lot of wisdom in his comment. Sullivan had an eye for talent and was a master at attracting talented people to his show. Many stand-up comics and musical groups who became famous in the 1960s can trace the beginning of their success back to an appearance on the *Ed Sullivan Show*. For your inner circle, value people capable of raising up others.

5. PROVEN VALUE—THOSE WHO RAISE UP PEOPLE WHO RAISE UP OTHER PEOPLE

The greatest value to any leader is someone who can raise up other leaders. That produces multigenerational leadership. (The power of this can be seen in the Law of Explosive Growth.)

NEVER STOP IMPROVING YOUR INNER CIRCLE

In my book *Developing the Leader Within You,* I wrote about how I reviewed my life when I turned forty. I had the desire to keep going to a higher level and to make a greater impact, but I realized that I had leveraged my time as much as I possibly could, and it would have been impossible to sharpen the focus on my priorities any more than it already was. In other words, I could not work harder *or* smarter. That left me only one choice: learning to work through others. That's the day I truly understood the Law of the Inner Circle. Since then, I have been committed to continually developing my inner circle. I hire the best staff I can find, develop them as much as I can, and hand off everything I possibly can.

In 1994, I discovered one of the key members of my inner circle. At the time, INJOY Stewardship Services (ISS), the second company I founded, was about two years old, and it wasn't doing all that well. It was succeeding in fulfilling its mission of capital campaign consulting, but it wasn't growing fast enough, and as a result, it was losing money. It needed a really good leader. Dick Peterson, the president of my first company, already had his hands full with INJOY. And I didn't have the time to lead it myself, with my heavy speaking schedule, a church of 3,500 (including a staff of forty), and a family with two kids in high school.

> *Hire the best staff you can find, develop them as much as you can, and hand off everything you possibly can to them.*

At that time, Dick and I decided to go to Seattle to seek advice from Dave Sutherland, an IBM executive with a remarkable marketing background, an intuitive leadership ability, and one of the finest strategic minds I've ever encountered. I already knew Dave casually, and he had some experience interacting with ISS, so he was willing to sit down and talk to me as a favor to a friend. Several weeks prior to the meeting, I filled him in on everything I thought he needed to know, and I asked him to think about what he would do if he were the one trying to take the company to the next level.

As we sat down in my hotel room in Seattle, he started to lay out an incredible strategy for ISS. He believed in our mission because we had helped his church and pastor earlier that year. And he knew exactly what it would take to move the company to the next level. After about thirty minutes, that's when it hit me. *Dave is the guy who can do it.*

"Dave," I said, "I want to hire *you* to run ISS." Dave ignored me and kept communicating the plan to me. About an hour later, I told him again, "Dave, I want to hire you." Again, he ignored me and kept telling Dick and me his plan. Finally, after we had been at it about four hours, I told him again. I said, "Dave, didn't you hear me? I'm telling you that I want to hire you to be the president of ISS. Why are you ignoring me?"

At that point, he finally took my request seriously. I realized that I didn't have much to offer Dave. He was one of the top guys in the country for IBM in its marketing area. And all I had was a small company and a dream. But because of the Law of the Inner Circle, I knew that my potential and that of my organizations would skyrocket if Dave became a part of my team. When I offered to give him my ISS salary if he came on board, he finally realized how serious I was. And though it meant taking a big pay cut, Dave took the job.

Today, ISS is the fastest growing company of its type and the second largest capital campaign consulting firm in the United States. It has gone to a whole new level, thanks to Dave Sutherland. And not only that, Dave brings his strategic thinking and marketing savvy to the table for all four of my companies.

Dave Sutherland is only one of a dozen or so key players that I've added to my inner circle. I've been strategically building that group for more than ten years—ever since my fortieth birthday. Dave is joined by INJOY President Dick Peterson and longtime colleagues Dan Reiland and Tim Elmore, who feel like my right and left hands when it comes to creating resources for leaders. The three of them have been with me for well over a decade. Other more recent additions include Ron McManus and Chris Fryer, my other two company presidents. My assistant, Linda Eggers, does the impossible with my calendar and organizational needs every day, while Charlie Wetzel, my writer, makes it possible for me to keep producing books despite my demanding schedule. Up-and-coming leaders like young managers Dave Johnson, Kevin Small, and Larry Figueroa are also helping INJOY make an incredible impact. And of course, I can't forget my good buddy Jim Dornan, my brother, Larry Maxwell, and my best friend in the whole world, Margaret, my wife.

Lee Iacocca says that success comes not from what you know, but from who you know and how you present yourself to each of those people. There is a lot of truth in that. I must say that I'm blessed with an incredible team. But I'm not finished yet. I'll continue building and adding good people for another decade and longer. You see, I know I have more potential that I haven't yet reached, and if I want someday to get there, I've got to surround myself with the best people possible. That's the only way it will ever happen. That's the Law of the Inner Circle.

THE LAW OF EMPOWERMENT

Only Secure Leaders Give Power to Others

J UST ABOUT EVERYBODY has heard of Henry Ford. He was the
revolutionary innovator in the automobile industry and a legend in
American business history. In 1903, he cofounded the Ford Motor
Company with the belief that the future of the automobile lay in
putting it within the reach of the average American. Ford said,

> I will build a motorcar for the multitude. It will be large enough
> for the family but small enough for the individual to run and
> care for. It will be constructed of the best materials, by the best
> men to be hired, after the simplest designs that modern engi-
> neering can devise. But it will be so low in price that no man
> making a good salary will be unable to own one—and enjoy
> with his family the blessings of hours of pleasure in God's great
> open spaces.

Henry Ford carried out that vision with the Model T, and it
changed the face of twentieth-century American life. By 1914,

Ford was producing nearly 50 percent of all automobiles in the United States. The Ford Motor Company looked like an American success story.

A LESS-KNOWN CHAPTER OF THE STORY

However, all of Ford's story is not about positive achievement, and one of the reasons was that he didn't embrace the Law of Empowerment. Henry Ford was so in love with his Model T that he never wanted to change or improve it—nor did he want anyone else to tinker with it. One day when a group of his designers surprised him by presenting him with the prototype of an improved model, Ford ripped its doors off the hinges and proceeded to destroy the car with his bare hands.

For almost twenty years, the Ford Motor Company offered only one design, the Model T, which Ford had personally developed. It wasn't until 1927 that he finally—grudgingly—agreed to offer a new car to the public. The company produced the Model A, but it was incredibly far behind its competitors in technical innovations. Despite its early head start and the incredible lead over its competitors, the Ford Motor Company's market share kept shrinking. By 1931, it was down to only 28 percent.

Henry Ford was the antithesis of an empowering leader. He always seemed to undermine his leaders and look over the shoulders of his people. He even created a sociological department within Ford Motor Company to check up on his employees and direct their private lives. And as time went by, he became more and more eccentric. He once went into his accounting office and tossed the company's books into the street, saying, "Just put all the money we take in in [*sic*] a big barrel and when a shipment of material comes in reach into the barrel and take out enough money to pay for it." He also devoted more and more of his time and money to pet projects, such as growing and experimenting with hundreds of varieties of soybeans.

Perhaps Ford's most peculiar dealings were with his executives, especially his son Edsel. The younger Ford had worked at the company since he was a boy. As Henry became more eccentric, Edsel worked harder to keep the company going. If it weren't for Edsel, the Ford Motor Company probably would have gone out of business in the 1930s. Henry eventually gave Edsel the presidency of the company and publicly said that Ford Motor Company's future looked bright with his leadership. Yet at the same time he undermined him and backed other leaders within the organization. Anytime a promising leader rose up in the company, Henry tore him down. As a result, the company kept losing its best executives. The few who stayed did so because of Edsel. They figured that someday old Henry would die, and Edsel would finally take over and set things right. But that's not what happened. In 1943, Edsel died at age forty-nine.

ANOTHER HENRY FORD

Edsel's oldest son, the twenty-six-year-old Henry Ford II, quickly left the navy so that he could return to Dearborn, Michigan, and take over the company. At first, he faced opposition from his grandfather's entrenched followers. But within two years, he gathered the support of several key people, received the backing of the board of directors (his mother controlled 41 percent of Ford Motor Company's stock), and convinced his grandfather to step down so that he could become president in his place.

Young Henry was taking over a company that hadn't made a profit in fifteen years. At that time, it was losing $1 million *a day!* The young president knew he was in over his head, so he began looking for leaders. Fortunately, the first group actually approached him. It was a team of ten men, headed by Colonel Charles "Tex" Thornton, who had decided they wanted to work together following their service at the War Department during World War II. Their contribution to Ford Motor Company was substantial. In the years to come, the group produced six company vice presidents and two presidents.

The second influx of leadership came with the entrance of Ernie Breech, an experienced General Motors executive and the former president of Bendix Aviation. Young Henry hired him to be Ford's executive vice president. Although Breech held a position second to Henry's, the expectation was that he would take command and turn the company around. And he did. Breech quickly brought in more than 150 outstanding executives from General Motors, and by 1949, Ford Motor Company was on a roll again. In that year, the company sold more than a million Fords, Mercurys, and Lincolns—the best sales since the Model A.

WHO'S THE BOSS?

If Henry Ford II had lived by the Law of Empowerment, the Ford Motor Company might have grown enough to eventually overtake General Motors and become the number one car company again. But only secure leaders are able to give power to others. Henry felt threatened. The success of Tex Thornton, Ernie Breech, and Lewis Crusoe, a legendary GM executive Breech had brought into the company, made Henry worry about his own place at Ford. His position was based not on influence but on his name and his family's control of company stock.

So Henry began pitting one top executive against another. He would invite Thornton to his office and encourage him to criticize fellow executive Crusoe. After a while, Crusoe got fed up with Thornton's insubordination and demanded that Breech fire him, which he did. Then Ford started backing Crusoe, who worked for Breech. Ford biographers Peter Collier and David Horowitz described the second Henry Ford's method this way:

Henry's instinct for survival manifested itself as craftiness combined with a kind of weakness. He had endowed Crusoe with the power to do virtually what ever he wished. By withdrawing his grace from Breech and bestowing it on his lieutenant, he had made antagonists of the two men most vital to Ford's success. While Henry had lost confidence in Breech, however, he had left him officially in charge because this increased his own maneuverability. And, as Crusoe's official superior, Breech could be useful if Henry wanted to keep Crusoe in check.[1]

> *"The best executive is the one who has sense enough to pick good men to do what he wants done, and self-restraint enough to keep from meddling with them while they do it."*
> —*Theodore Roosevelt*

This became a pattern in the leadership of Henry Ford II. Anytime an executive gained power and influence, Henry undercut the person's authority by moving him to a position with less clout, supporting the executive's subordinates, or publicly humiliating him. This continued all the days Henry II was at Ford. As one Ford president, Lee Iacocca, commented after leaving the company, "Henry Ford, as I would learn firsthand, had a nasty habit of getting rid of strong leaders."

IF YOU CAN'T LEAD 'EM . . .

Iacocca said that Henry Ford II once described his leadership philosophy to him, years before Iacocca himself became its target. Ford said, "If a guy works for you, don't let him get too comfortable. Don't let him get cozy or set in his ways. Always do the opposite of what he expects. Keep your people anxious and off-balance."[2]

Both Henry Fords failed to abide by the Law of Empowerment. Rather than finding leaders, building them up, giving them resources, authority, and responsibility, and then turning them loose to achieve, they alternately encouraged and undermined their best people because of their own insecurity. But if you want to be successful as a leader, you have to be an empowerer. Theodore Roosevelt realized that, "the best executive is the one who has sense enough to pick good men to do what he wants done, and the self-restraint enough to keep from meddling with them while they do it."

BARRIERS TO EMPOWERMENT

Leadership analysts Lynne McFarland, Larry Senn, and John Childress affirm that "the empowerment leadership model shifts away from 'position power' where all people are given leadership roles so they can contribute to their fullest capacity."[3] Only empowered people can reach their potential. When a leader can't or won't empower others, he creates barriers within the organization that people cannot overcome. If the barriers remain long enough, then the people give up, or they move to another organization where they can maximize their potential.

> *The people's capacity to achieve is determined by their leader's ability to empower.*

Why do some leaders violate the Law of Empowerment? Consider some common reasons:

DESIRE FOR JOB SECURITY

The number one enemy of empowerment is the desire for job security. A weak leader worries that if he helps subordinates, he will become dispensable. But the truth is that the only way to make yourself indispensable is to make yourself dispensable. In other words, if you are able to continually empower others and help them develop so that they become capable of taking over your job, you will become so valuable to the organization that you become indispensable. That's a paradox of the Law of Empowerment.

> *The only way to make yourself indispensable is to make yourself dispensable.*

RESISTANCE TO CHANGE

Nobel Prize–winning author John Steinbeck asserted, "It is the nature of man as he grows older to protest against change, particularly change for the better." By its very nature, empowerment brings constant change because it encourages people to grow and innovate. Change is the price of progress.

LACK OF SELF-WORTH

Many people gain their personal value and esteem from their work or position. Threaten to change either of them, and you threaten their self-worth. On the other hand, author Buck Rogers says, "To those who have confidence in themselves, change is a stimulus because they believe one person can make a difference and influence what goes on around them. These people are the doers and motivators." They are also the empowerers.

LEADING BY LIFTING UP OTHERS

Only secure leaders are able to give themselves away. Mark Twain once remarked that great things can happen when you don't care who gets the credit. But you can take that a step farther. I believe the greatest things happen *only* when you give others the credit. That's the Law of Empowerment in action. One-time vice presidential candidate Admiral James B. Stockdale declared, "Leadership must be based on goodwill . . . It means obvious and wholehearted commitment to helping followers . . . What we need for leaders are men of heart who are so helpful that they, in effect, do away with the need of their jobs.

But leaders like that are never out of a job, never out of followers. Strange as it sounds, great leaders gain authority by giving it away."

One of the greatest leaders of this nation was truly gifted at giving his power and authority to others. His name was Abraham Lincoln. The depth of Lincoln's security as a leader can be seen in the selection of his cabinet. Most presidents pick like-minded allies. But not Lincoln. At a time of turmoil for the country when disparate voices were many, Lincoln brought together a group of leaders who would unify his party and bring strength through diversity and mutual challenge. One Lincoln biographer said this of his method:

> *The greatest things happen only when you give others the credit.*

For a President to select a political rival for a cabinet post was not unprecedented; but deliberately to surround himself with all of his disappointed antagonists seemed to be courting disaster. It was a mark of his sincere intentions that Lincoln wanted the advice of men as strong as himself or stronger. That he entertained no fear of being crushed or overridden by such men revealed either surpassing naïveté or a tranquil confidence in his powers of leadership.[4]

Lincoln lived the Law of Empowerment. His security enabled him to give his power away.

FINDING STRONG LEADERS TO EMPOWER

Lincoln's ability to empower played a major role in his relationship with his generals during the Civil War. In the beginning, he had trouble finding worthy recipients of his confidence. When the Southern states seceded, the finest generals in the land went south to serve the Confederacy. But Lincoln never lost hope, nor did he neglect to give his leaders power and freedom, even when that strategy had failed with previous generals.

For example, in June of 1863, Lincoln put the command of the Army of the Potomac into the hands of General George G. Meade. Lincoln hoped that he would do a better job than had preceding generals Ambrose E. Burnside and Joseph Hooker. Within hours of Meade's appointment, Lincoln sent a courier to him. The president's message, in part, said,

> Considering the circumstances, no one ever received a more important command; and I cannot doubt that you will fully justify the confidence which the Government has reposed in you. You will not be hampered by any minute instructions from these headquarters. Your army is free to act as you may deem proper under the circumstances as they arise . . . All forces within the sphere of your operations will be held subject to your orders.[5]

As it turned out, Meade's first significant challenge came as he commanded the army at a small Pennsylvania town named Gettysburg. It was a test he passed with authority. In the end, though, Meade was not the general who would make full use of the power Lincoln offered. It took Ulysses S. Grant to turn the war around. But Meade stopped Lee's army when it counted, and he prevented the Confederate general from moving on Washington.

To push people down, you have to go down with them.

Lincoln's use of the Law of Empowerment was as consistent as Henry Ford's habit of breaking it. Even when his generals performed poorly, Lincoln took the blame. Lincoln expert Donald T. Phillips acknowledged, "Throughout the war Lincoln continued to accept public responsibility for battles lost or opportunities missed."[6]

Lincoln was able to stand strongly during the war and continually give power to others because of his rock-solid security.

THE POWER OF EMPOWERMENT

A key to empowering others is high belief in people. I feel I've been fortunate because believing in others has always been very easy for me. I recently received a note from the one person, outside my family, whom I have worked hardest to empower. His name is Dan Reiland. He was my executive pastor when I was at Skyline, and today he is the vice president for leadership development at INJOY. Dan wrote,

> John,
> The ultimate in mentoring has come to pass. I am being asked to teach on the topic of empowerment! I can do this only because you first empowered me. The day is still crystal clear in my mind when you took a risk and chose me as your Executive Pastor. You trusted me with significant responsibility, the day to day leadership of the staff and ministries of your church. You released me with authority . . . You believed in me—perhaps more than I believed in myself. You demonstrated your faith and confidence in me in such a way that I could tap into your belief, and eventually it became my own . . .
> I am so very grateful for your life-changing impact on my life. Saying thank you hardly touches it. "I love and appreciate you" is better. Perhaps the best way I can show my gratitude is to pass on the gift you have given me to other leaders in my life.
> Dan

I am grateful to Dan for all he has done for me, and I believe he has returned to me much more than I have given to him. And I've genuinely enjoyed the time I've spent with Dan helping him grow. The truth is that empowerment is powerful—not only for the person being developed, but also for the mentor. Enlarging others makes you larger. Dan has made me better than I am, not just because he helped me achieve much more than I could have done on my own, but also because the whole process made me a better leader. That is the impact of the Law of Empowerment.

THE LAW OF REPRODUCTION

It Takes a Leader to Raise Up a Leader

T HIS YEAR IN MY leadership conferences, I've been taking time to conduct an informal poll to find out what prompted the men and women who attend to become leaders. The results of the survey are as follows:

HOW THEY BECAME LEADERS

Natural Gifting	10 percent
Result of Crisis	5 percent
Influence of Another Leader	85 percent

If you've ever given much thought to the origins of leadership, then you're probably not surprised by those figures. It's true that a few people step into leadership because their organization experiences a crisis, and they are compelled to do something about it. Another small group is comprised of people with such great natural gifting and instincts that they are able to navigate their way into leadership on their own. But more than four out of five of all the leaders that you ever meet will have emerged as leaders because of the impact made on them by established leaders who mentored them. That happens because of the Law of Reproduction: It takes a leader to raise up a leader.

MANY FOLLOW IN THEIR FOOTSTEPS

Of the people I surveyed, about one-third are leaders in the business world and two-thirds are leaders in churches. But the responses will be similar in just about any field. For instance, you will find the Law of Reproduction at work in professional football. Let me ask you this: Did you know that the development and mentoring of half of the head coaches in the NFL (in 1998) can be traced to two outstanding former pro football leaders—Bill Walsh and Tom Landry? Ten current NFL head coaches spent a year or longer working for three-time Super Bowl–champion Bill Walsh or for one of the top assistants he trained. And five NFL coaches have a direct or indirect mentoring connection with two-time Super Bowl–winner Tom Landry or one of the men he trained.

Just about every successful coach in the NFL has spent time working with another strong leader who helped to teach and model for him. In addition to the ones with a Walsh or Landry connection, there are other NFL examples: Dave Wannstedt worked for two-time Super Bowl–champion Jimmy Johnson, and head coaches Bill Cowher and Tony Dungy spent significant time working with Marty Schottenheimer of the Kansas City Chiefs. It takes a leader to raise up a leader.

SOME DO IT, SOME DON'T

In the chapter on the Law of Respect, I explained that people naturally follow leaders stronger than themselves. In the same way, only leaders

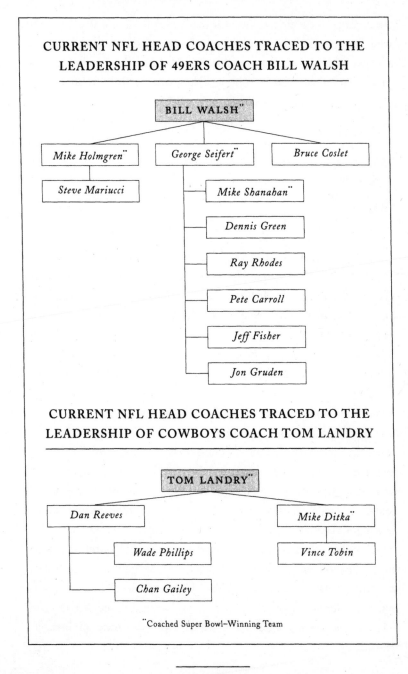

CURRENT NFL HEAD COACHES TRACED TO THE LEADERSHIP OF 49ERS COACH BILL WALSH

BILL WALSH¨

Mike Holmgren¨   George Seifert¨   Bruce Coslet

Steve Mariucci   Mike Shanahan¨

Dennis Green

Ray Rhodes

Pete Carroll

Jeff Fisher

Jon Gruden

CURRENT NFL HEAD COACHES TRACED TO THE LEADERSHIP OF COWBOYS COACH TOM LANDRY

TOM LANDRY¨

Dan Reeves   Mike Ditka¨

Wade Phillips   Vince Tobin

Chan Gailey

¨Coached Super Bowl–Winning Team

are capable of developing other leaders. People cannot give to others what they themselves do not possess. Followers simply cannot develop leaders. But just because a person is a leader, it does not necessarily mean that he will raise up other leaders. For every Bill Walsh, George Seifert, or Tom Landry, there is a Vince Lombardi—a person who is a great coach and leader in his own right, but who doesn't raise up other great coaches to follow in his footsteps.

> *People cannot give to others what they themselves do not possess. Followers simply cannot develop leaders.*

Why don't all leaders develop others? There are many reasons. Sometimes they just don't recognize the tremendous *value* of developing leaders. (I'll talk more about that value in the chapter on the Law of Explosive Growth.) Others may focus so much attention on their followers and give them so much that they don't have anything left for their key staff. I suspect that was the case with Vince Lombardi. For other leaders the real problem may be insecurity. Remember what the Law of Empowerment teaches: Only secure leaders give power to others.

As a kid, did you ever play follow the leader? I know I did. Even then I wanted to be the leader. Do you remember what you had to do to stay in front in that game? You purposely tried to get your followers to make mistakes. That's what sent them to the back of the line. The same thing was true when playing the game of horse on the basketball court. You made your shots so hard that others couldn't possibly duplicate them. And if you were like me, you had a special home-court, failsafe shot that no other kid could make, and you used it to put the game away. The problem with the old follow-the-leader games is that to win, you had to make the other guy lose. That's opposite of the way you raise up leaders.

Last year as I conducted a leadership conference in Jakarta,

Indonesia, I taught the Law of Reproduction and talked about the follow-the-leader game. I asked a volunteer to come up so that I could show visually what happens when a leader tries to keep others down instead of raising them up. I had the volunteer stand in front of me, and I put my hands on his shoulders. Then I began pushing him down. The lower I wanted to push him, the more I had to bend down to do it. The lower I wanted him to go, the lower I had to go. That's the same way it is in leadership: to keep others down, you have to go down with them.

RAISING UP GIANT KILLERS

One of my favorite stories that illustrates the Law of Reproduction is about David of ancient Israel. Just about everyone has heard the story of David and Goliath. When the armies of the Philistines faced off against King Saul and the people of Israel, Goliath, a large, powerful professional warrior, laid out a challenge. He said he'd fight Israel's greatest champion in a winner-take-all battle. And who stepped forward to accept the challenge? Not Saul, the mighty king, or any of his seasoned veterans. David, a lowly shepherd boy, stood to face him, and using a sling, he hurled a rock at Goliath, knocked him out, and then cut the big warrior's head off with Goliath's own sword.

We all identify with a story like that because we like to cheer for the underdog. But many people don't know the rest of the story. David grew up to be a warrior and eventually became king. But along the way, he raised up a group of great warriors who were called his "mighty men." No fewer than five of them also became giant killers, just like their leader. Had Saul, the previous king, done that? No. It took a person who had done it himself. And just as it takes a giant killer to produce other giant killers, it takes a leader to raise up other leaders.

WE TEACH WHAT WE KNOW—
WE REPRODUCE WHAT WE ARE

I was very fortunate growing up because I lived in the household of a leader: my father, Melvin Maxwell. Every day of my early life, I learned lessons about working with people, understanding priorities, developing myself through a personal growth plan, and paying the price of leadership. Some of what I learned came from his teaching. But even more of it came from being around him, watching him interact with others, and learning how he thought. As a result, by the time I went to college, I already had pretty good intuition and under-stood leadership better than most of my peers did. Since then, I've continued to learn about leadership. And I've sought out great leaders to mentor me so that I can keep learning.

> *Just as it takes a giant killer to produce other giant killers, it takes a leader to raise up other leaders.*

If you want to continue developing as a leader, you should do the same. Spend time with the best leaders you can find. If you're just starting out, you may want to spend time with people in your field so that you can master the basics of your profession. But once you have that foundation, learn leadership from people in many professions. I've learned from businesspeople, pas-tors, politicians, generals, ballplayers, entrepreneurs—you name it. No matter what the profession, the principles of leadership remain the same.

Not everyone understands that immediately. For example, sev-eral years ago when I told my brother, Larry, that I was going to start spending more time teaching leadership in the corporate world, he was a little skeptical. Larry is a natural businessman. He achieved financial independence in real estate by the time he was in his twenties, and he sits on several corporate boards and is a trustee of one university. But he wasn't sure if businesspeople would be receptive to learning leadership from someone with a pastoral background. But I knew that leadership is leadership; the principles apply no matter where you are. And sure enough, when I started teaching leadership to organizations such as Sam's Club, Wal-Mart, Mary Kay, and Baillie Lumber—and the people saw that the principles worked—they kept asking for more. Why would such big companies seek advice from someone who leads four small companies? Because they understand the Law of Reproduction. They know that it takes a leader to raise up other leaders—no matter the field.

TAKE THE NEXT STEP

The only way you will be able to develop other leaders is to become a better leader yourself. If you've already taken those first steps, you are to be commended. You're in a position to begin raising up other leaders. As you get started, keep in mind that leaders who develop leaders . . .

SEE THE BIG PICTURE

Every effective leadership mentor makes the development of leaders one of his highest priorities in life. He knows that the potential of the organization depends on the growth of its leadership. The more leaders there are, the greater its chance of success.

ATTRACT POTENTIAL LEADERS

You've probably heard the Ross Perot quote: "Leaders don't flock. You have to find them one at a time." That's true. But as the Law of Magnetism also suggests, if you first develop your leadership qualities, you will be capable of attracting people with leadership potential. When you do that and also earn their respect, you will get the opportunity to develop them into better leaders.

CREATE AN EAGLE ENVIRONMENT

An environment where leadership is valued and taught becomes an asset to a leadership mentor. It not only attracts "eagles," but it also helps them learn to fly. An eagle environment is one where the leader casts a vision, offers incentives, encourages creativity, allows risks, and provides accountability. Do that long enough with enough people, and you'll develop a leadership culture where eagles begin to flock.

THE IMPACT CARRIES OVER

Once you understand the Law of Reproduction, you recognize its incredible impact on an organization. If a company has poor leaders, what little leadership it has will only get worse. If a company has strong leaders—and they are reproducing themselves—then the leadership just keeps getting better and better.

Occasionally, a company will emerge where the leadership is so strong and the development process is so deliberate that the impact not only drives that organization to the highest level, but it also over-flows into other businesses. That is the case at General Electric, led by chairman Jack Welch. GE has become one of the best-run com-panies in the world, and it keeps developing leader upon leader. In fact, the company has *lost* more leaders capable of running organiza-tions than most other good companies are able to produce in their lifetimes. Scan this list of CEOs who once worked at GE:

> William Anders, *General Dynamics*
> Norman P. Blake Jr., *USF&G*
> Larry A. Bossidy, *Allied-Signal Inc.*
> Michael J. Emmi, *Systems and Computer Technology*
> Stanley C. Gault, *Rubbermaid Inc.*, and later,
>   *Goodyear Tire and Rubber Corp.*

Fred Garry, *late chief executive of Rohr Inc.*
Robert Goldsmith, *former chief executive, Rohr Inc.*
Glen Hiner, *Owens Corning Fiberglass*
Clyde Keaton, *Clean Harbors*
Chuck Lillis, *MediaOne Group*
    (formerly *U.S. West Media Group*)
Michael Lockhart, *General Signal Corp.*
Daniel McClaughlin, *Equifax*
Richard Miller, *Wang Laboratories*
George Schofield, *Zurn Industries*
Roger Shipke, *Ryland Group Inc.*
Harry C. Stonecipher, *Sunstrand,* and later,
    McDonnell Douglas Corp.
John M. Trani, *Stanley Works*
Walter Williams, *Rubbermaid*
Thomas Vanderslice, *president of GTE,* then *CEO for*
    Apollo Computer, and then *CEO of M/A Com,*
    which produces microwave components
Alva O. Way, *American Express Co.*

Just as in the world of pro football, the ability of many leaders can be traced to a common source. How was General Electric able to produce so many outstanding leaders? First, leadership development is one of the company's highest priorities. It spends more than $500 million a year on training and develops leaders at its own institute in Crotonville, often called "the Harvard of corporate America."[1] But even more important than that is the fact that the company is run by a great leader, Jack Welch.

It all starts at the top because it takes a leader to raise up another leader. Followers can't do it. Neither can institutional programs. It takes one to know one, show one, and grow one. That's the Law of Reproduction.

14

THE LAW OF BUY-IN

People Buy Into the Leader, Then the Vision

I N THE FALL OF 1997, a few members of my staff and I had the opportunity to travel to India and teach four leadership conferences. India is an amazing country, full of contradictions. It's a place of beauty with warm and generous people, yet at the same time millions and millions of its inhabitants live in the worst poverty imaginable. It was there that I was reminded of the Law of Buy-In.

I'll never forget when our plane landed in Delhi. Exiting the airport, I felt as if we had been transported to another planet. There were crowds everywhere. People on bicycles, in cars, on camels and elephants. People on the streets, some sleeping right on the sidewalks. Animals roamed free, no matter where we were. And everything was in motion. As we drove along the main street toward our hotel, I also noticed something else. Banners. Wherever we looked, we could see banners celebrating India's fifty years of liberty, along with huge pictures of one man: Mahatma Gandhi.

Today, people take for granted that Gandhi was a great leader. But the story of his leadership is a marvelous study in the Law of Buy-In.

Mohandas K. Gandhi, called Mahatma (which means "great soul"), was educated in London. After finishing his education in law, he traveled back to India and then to South Africa. There he worked for twenty years as a barrister and political activist. And in that time he developed as a leader, fighting for the rights of Indians and other minorities who were oppressed and discriminated against by South Africa's apartheid government.

By the time he returned to India in 1914, Gandhi was very well known and highly respected among his countrymen. Over the next several years, as he led protests and strikes around the country, people rallied to him and looked to him more and more for leadership. In 1920—a mere six years after returning to India—he was elected president of the All India Home Rule League.

The most remarkable thing about Gandhi isn't that he became their leader, but that he was able to change the people's vision for obtaining freedom. Before he began leading them, the people used violence in an effort to achieve their goals. For years riots against the British establishment had been common. But Gandhi's vision for change in India was based on nonviolent civil disobedience. He once said, "Nonviolence is the greatest force at the disposal of mankind. It is mightier than the mightiest weapon of destruction devised by the ingenuity of man."

Gandhi challenged the people to meet oppression with peaceful disobedience and noncooperation. Even when the British military massacred more than one thousand people at Amritsar in 1919, Gandhi called the people to stand, but without fighting back. Rallying everyone to his way of thinking wasn't easy. But because the people had come to buy into him as their leader, they embraced his vision. And then they followed him faithfully. He asked them not to fight, and eventually, they stopped fighting. When he called for everyone to burn foreign-made clothes and start wearing nothing but home-spun material, millions of people started doing it. When he decided that a March to the Sea to protest the Salt Act would be their rallying point for civil disobedience against the British, the nation's leaders followed him the two hundred miles to the city of Dandi, where they were arrested by government representatives.

Their struggle for independence was slow and painful, but Gandhi's leadership was strong enough to deliver on the promise of his vision. In 1947, India gained home rule. Because the people had bought into Gandhi, they accepted his vision. And once they had embraced the vision, they were able to carry it out. That's how the Law of Buy-In works. The leader finds the dream and then the people. The people find the leader, and then the dream.

> *The leader finds the dream and then the people. The people find the leader and then the dream.*

DON'T PUT THE CART FIRST

When I teach leadership seminars, I field a lot of questions about vision. Invariably someone will come up to me during a break, give me a brief description of an evolving vision, and ask me, "Do you think my people will buy into my vision?" My response is always the same: "First tell me this. Do your people buy into you?"

You see, many people who approach the area of vision in leadership have it all backward. They believe that if the cause is good enough, people will automatically buy into it and follow. But that's not how leadership really works. People don't at first follow worthy causes. They follow worthy leaders who promote worthwhile causes. People buy into the leader first, then the leader's vision. Having an understanding of that changes your whole approach to leading people.

For the person who attends one of my conferences and asks whether his people will follow, the question really becomes, "Have I given my people reasons to buy into me?" If his answer is yes, they will gladly buy into his vision. But if he has not built his credibility with his people, it really doesn't matter how great a vision he has.

> *People don't at first follow worthy causes. They follow worthy leaders who promote worthwhile causes.*

Not long ago I was reading an article in *Business Week* that profiled entrepreneurs who partner with venture capitalists in the computer industry. Silicon Valley in California is evidently full of people who work in the computer industry for a while and then try to start their own companies. Every day hundreds of them are buzzing around trying to find investors so that they can get their ideas and enterprises off the ground. Many are unsuccessful. But if an entrepreneur succeeds once, then he finds it pretty easy to find money the next time around. Many times, the investors aren't even interested in finding out what the entrepreneur's vision is. If they've bought into the person, then they readily accept the ideas.

For example, software entrepreneur Judy Estrim and her partner have founded two companies over the years. She said that funding her first company took six months and countless presentations, even though she had a viable idea and believed in it 100 percent. But the start-up of her second company happened almost overnight. It took only two phone calls that lasted mere minutes for her to land $5 million in backing. When the word got out that she was starting her second company, people were dying to give her even more money. She said, "We had venture capitalists calling us and begging us to take their money."[1] Why had everything changed so drastically for her? Because of the Law of Buy-In. People had bought into her, so they were ready to buy into whatever vision she offered, sight unseen.

YOU ARE THE MESSAGE

Every message that people receive is filtered through the messenger who delivers it. If you consider the messenger to be credible, then you believe the message has value. That's one of the reasons actors and athletes are hired as promoters of products. People buy Nike shoes because they have bought into Michael Jordan, not necessarily because of the quality of the shoes. The same is true when actors promote causes. Have the actors being employed suddenly become experts in the cause they're promoting? Usually not. But that doesn't matter. People want to listen to Charlton Heston as he speaks for the NRA, not because they believe he is an expert in the field of hunting or guns, but because they believe in him as a person and because he has credibility as an actor. Once people have bought into someone, they are willing to give his vision a chance. People want to go along with people they get along with.

> *People want to go along with people they get along with.*

IT'S NOT AN EITHER/OR PROPOSITION

You cannot separate the leader from the cause he promotes. It cannot be done, no matter how hard you try. It's not an either/or proposition. The two always go together. Take a look at the following table. It shows how people react to a leader and his vision under different circumstances:

LEADER	+	VISION	=	RESULT
Don't Buy In		*Don't Buy In*		*Get Another Leader*
Don't Buy In		*Buy In*		*Get Another Leader*
Buy In		*Don't Buy In*		*Get Another Vision*
Buy In		*Buy In*		*Get Behind the Leader*

WHEN FOLLOWERS DON'T LIKE THE LEADER OR THE VISION, THEY LOOK FOR ANOTHER LEADER

It's easy to understand the reaction of people when they don't like the leader or the vision. They don't follow. But they also do something else: They start looking for another leader. It's a no-win situation.

WHEN FOLLOWERS DON'T LIKE THE LEADER BUT THEY DO LIKE THE VISION, THEY STILL LOOK FOR ANOTHER LEADER

You may be surprised by this. Even though people may think a cause is good, if they don't like the leader, they will go out and find another one. That's one reason that coaches change teams so often in professional sports. The vision for any team always stays the same: Everyone wants to win a championship. But the players don't always believe in their leader. And when they don't, what happens? The owners don't fire all of the players. They fire the leader and bring in someone they hope the players will buy into.

WHEN FOLLOWERS LIKE THE LEADER BUT NOT THE VISION, THEY CHANGE THE VISION

Even when people don't like a leader's vision, if they've already bought into him, they will keep following him. You often see this response in politics. For example, in the past, the National Organization of Women (NOW) has spoken out strongly against sexual harassment. But recently when Paula Jones accused President Clinton of sexually harassing her, NOW continued to support him. Why? It's not because the members suddenly think sexual harassment is acceptable. They have chosen to put their agenda on hold in order to keep supporting the leader they've already bought into.

When followers don't agree with their leader's vision, they react in many ways. Sometimes they work to convince their leader to change his vision. Sometimes they abandon their point of view and adopt his. Other times they find a compromise. But as long as they still buy into the leader, they won't out-and-out reject him. They will keep following.

WHEN FOLLOWERS LIKE THE LEADER AND THE VISION, THEY WILL GET BEHIND BOTH

They will follow their leader no matter how bad conditions get or how much the odds are stacked against them. That's why the Indian people in Gandhi's day refused to fight back as soldiers mowed them down. That's what inspired the U.S. space program to fulfill John F. Kennedy's vision and put a man on the moon. That's the reason people continued to have hope and keep alive the dream of Martin Luther King Jr., even after he was gunned down. That's what continues to inspire followers to keep running the race, even when they feel they've hit the wall and given everything they've got.

As a leader, having a great vision and a worthy cause is not enough to get people to follow you. First you have to become a better leader; you must get your people to buy into *you*. That is the price you have to pay if you want your vision to have a chance of becoming a reality.

BUYING TIME FOR PEOPLE TO BUY IN

If in the past you tried to get your people to act on your vision but were unable to make it happen, you probably came up against the Law of Buy-In, maybe without even knowing it. I first recognized the importance of the Law of Buy-In in 1972 when I accepted my second leadership position. In the chapter on the Law of Navigation, I mentioned that after I had been at that church several years, I took them through a multimillion-dollar construction program in which we built a new auditorium. But when I first got there, that was not the direction that the congregation had wanted to go.

The week before I arrived at my new church, more than 65 percent of the members had voted in favor of building a new activity center. Now, I had done some homework on that church, and I knew coming in that its future growth and success depended not on a new activity center, but on a new auditorium. My vision for the years ahead was absolutely clear to me. But I couldn't walk in and say, "Forget the decision you just made and all the agonizing you did to make it. Follow me instead." I needed to buy some time to build my credibility with the people.

I arranged for a committee to make a thorough study of all the issues involved with the activity center project. I told the members, "If we're going to invest this kind of time and money, we have to be sure about it. I must have information on every possible issue related to it." That seemed fair enough to everyone, and off the committee went to work. For the next year, the group would come back to me every month or so and report on the information gathered. And each time I'd praise their work and ask several questions that would prompt them to do more research.

In the meantime, I worked hard to build my credibility with the people. I forged relationships with the leaders in the church. I answered everybody's questions so that they could understand me and how I thought as a leader. I shared my ideas, hopes, and dreams for the work we were doing. And I started to produce growth in the organization. That, more than anything else, gave the people confidence in me and my ability.

After about six months, the people started to see that the church was changing and beginning to move in a new direction. In a year, the building committee decided that the activity center was not in the church's best interest, and they recommended that we not build it. In another year, the people had reached consensus: The key to the future was the building of a new auditorium. And when the time came, 98 percent of the people voted yes on the issue, and off we went.

When I arrived at that church, I could have tried to push my vision and agenda on the people. I was just as sure that it was the right thing to do in 1972 as I was two years later when we implemented it. But if I had approached it in that way, I wouldn't have succeeded in helping those people get where they needed to go. And in the process I would have undermined my ability to lead them.

As a leader, you don't earn any points for failing in a noble cause. You don't get credit for being "right." Your success is measured by your ability to actually take the people where they need to go. But you can do that only if the people first buy into you as a leader. That's the reality of the Law of Buy-In.

THE LAW OF VICTORY

Leaders Find a Way for the Team to Win

HAVE YOU EVER THOUGHT about what separates the leaders who achieve victory from those who suffer defeat? What does it take to be a winner? It's hard to put a finger on the quality that separates a winner from a loser. Every leadership situation is different. Every crisis has its own challenges. But I think that victorious leaders share an inability to accept defeat. The alternative to winning seems totally unacceptable to them, so they figure out what must be done to achieve victory, and then they go after it with everything at their disposal.

> *Victorious leaders feel the alternative to winning is totally unacceptable, so they figure out what must be done to achieve victory, and then they go after it with everything at their disposal.*

I'm a Civil War buff, and I was reading an old book that reminded me of the importance of the Law of Victory. It discussed the differences between the presidents of the Union and the Confederacy: Abraham Lincoln and Jefferson Davis. I've talked quite a bit about

Lincoln throughout *The 21 Irrefutable Laws of Leadership* because he was such a remarkable leader. Lincoln never forgot that the nation's victory was his highest priority, ahead of his pride, reputation, and personal comfort. He surrounded himself with the best leaders possible, empowered his generals, and was never afraid to give others the credit for the victories the Union gained. For example, following General Grant's victory at Vicksburg, Lincoln sent a letter to him saying, "I never had any faith, except the general hope that you knew better than I . . . I now wish to make the personal acknowledgment that you were right and I was wrong."

Jefferson Davis, on the other hand, never seemed to make victory his priority. When he should have been thinking like a revolutionary, he worked like a bureaucrat. When he should have been delegating authority and decision making to his generals—the best in the land—he spent his time micromanaging them. And worst of all, he was more concerned with being right than with winning the war. Historian David M. Potter says of Davis, "He used an excessive share of his energy in contentious and even litigious argument to prove he was right. He seemed to feel that if he were right that was enough; that it was more important to vindicate his own rectitude than to get results."[1] Davis violated the Law of Victory, and as a consequence, his people suffered a devastating defeat.

THESE LEADERS PURSUED VICTORY

Crisis seems to bring out the best—and the worst—in leaders. During World War II, two outstanding leaders who practiced the Law of Victory emerged for the Allies: British Prime Minister Winston Churchill and U.S. President Franklin Roosevelt. They prevented Adolf Hitler from crushing Europe and remaking it according to his own vision.

On his side of the Atlantic Ocean, Winston Churchill inspired the British people to resist Hitler. Long before he became prime minister in 1940, Churchill spoke out against the Nazis. He seemed like the lone critic in 1932 when he warned, "Do not delude yourselves . . . Do not believe that all Germany is asking for is equal status . . . They are looking for weapons and when they have them believe me they will ask for the return of lost territories or colonies."

Churchill continued to speak out against the Nazis. And when Hitler annexed Austria in 1938, Churchill said to members of the House of Commons:

For five years I have talked to the House on these matters—not with very great success. I have watched this famous island descending incontinently, fecklessly, the stairway which leads to a dark gulf . . . Now is the time at last to rouse the nation. Perhaps it is the last time it can be roused with a chance of preventing war, or with a chance of coming through with victory should our effort to prevent war fail.

Unfortunately, Prime Minister Neville Chamberlain and the other leaders of Great Britain did not make a stand against Hitler. And more of Europe fell to the Nazis.

By mid-1940, most of Europe was under Germany's thumb. But then something happened that might have changed the history of the free world. The leadership of England fell to Winston Churchill. He refused to buckle under the Nazis' threats. For more than a year, Great Britain stood alone facing the threat of German invasion. When Hitler indicated that he wanted to make a deal with England, Churchill defied him. When Germany began bombing England, the British stood strong. And all the while, Churchill looked for a way to gain victory.

CHURCHILL WOULD ACCEPT NOTHING LESS

Time after time, Churchill rallied the British people. It began with his first speech after becoming prime minister:

> We have before us an ordeal of the most grievous kind. We have before us many, many long months of struggle and of suffering. You ask what is our policy? I will say: It is to wage war, by sea, land and air, with all our might and with all the strength that God can give us; to wage war against a monstrous tyranny, never surpassed in the dark, lamentable catalogue of human crime. That is our policy. You ask, What is our aim? I answer in one word: Victory—victory at all costs, victory in spite of all terror, victory, however long and hard the road may be; for without victory, there is no survival.[2]

Meanwhile, Churchill did everything in his power to prevail. He deployed troops in the Mediterranean against Mussolini's forces. Although he hated communism, he allied himself with Stalin and the Soviets, sending them aid even when Great Britain's supplies were threatened and its survival hung in the balance. And he developed his personal relationship with Franklin Roosevelt. Though the president of the United States was reluctant to enter the war, Churchill worked to build his relationship with him, hoping to change it from one of friendship and mutual respect to a full-fledged war alliance. In time his efforts paid off. On the day the Japanese bombed Pearl Harbor, ushering the United States into the war, Churchill said to himself, "So we have won after all."

> *"What is our aim? I answer in one word: Victory— victory at all costs, victory in spite of all terror, victory, however long and hard the road may be; for without victory, there is no survival."*
> —*Winston Churchill*

ANOTHER LEADER DEDICATED TO VICTORY

Prior to December 1941, Franklin Roosevelt had already been practicing the Law of Victory for decades. In fact, it is a hallmark of his
entire life. He had found a way to achieve political victory while
winning over polio. When he was elected president and became
responsible for pulling the American people out of the Great
Depression, it was just another impossible situation that he learned
how to fight through. And fight he did. Through the 1930s, the
country was slowly recovering.

By the time the Nazis were battling in Europe, the stakes were
high. Pulitzer Prize–winning historian Arthur Schlesinger Jr.,
noted, "The Second World War found democracy fighting for its
life. By 1941, there were only a dozen or so democratic states left on
earth. But great leadership emerged in time to rally the democratic
cause." The team of Roosevelt and Churchill provided that leadership like a one-two punch. Just as the prime minister had rallied
England, the president brought together the American people and
united them in a common cause as no one ever had before or has
since.

To those two leaders, victory was the only option. If they had
accepted anything less, the world would be a very different place
today. Schlesinger says, "Take a look at our present world. It is manifestly not Adolf Hitler's world. His Thousand-Year Reich turned
out to have a brief and bloody run of a dozen years. It is manifestly
not Joseph Stalin's world. That ghastly world self-destructed before
our eyes. Nor is it Winston Churchill's world . . . The world we live
in is Franklin Roosevelt's world."[3] Without Churchill and England,
all of Europe would have fallen. Without Roosevelt and the United
States, it might never have been reclaimed for freedom. But not even
an Adolf Hitler and the army of the Third Reich could stand against
two leaders dedicated to the Law of Victory.

GREAT LEADERS FIND A WAY TO WIN

When the pressure is on, great leaders are at their best. Whatever is inside them comes to the surface and works for or against them. Just a few years ago, Nelson Mandela was elected president of South Africa. It was a huge victory for the people of that country, but it was a long time coming. The road to that victory was paved with twenty-seven years of Mandela's own life spent in prison. Along the way, he did whatever it took to bring victory one step closer. He joined the African National Congress, which became an outlawed organization. He staged peaceful protests. He went underground and traveled overseas to try to enlist support. When he needed to, he stood trial and accepted a prison sentence, with dignity and courage. And when the time was right, he negotiated changes in the government with F. W. de Klerk. Today he is working to bring lasting victory by trying to bring healing to the country. Mandela describes himself as "an ordinary man who had become a leader because of extraordinary circumstances."[4] I say he is a leader made extraordinary because of the strength of his character and his dedication to the Law of Victory.

> *When the pressure is on, great leaders are at their best. Whatever is inside them comes to the surface.*

YOU CAN SEE IT EVERY DAY

You can readily see the Law of Victory in action at sporting events. In other areas of life, leaders do most of their work behind the scenes, and you never get to see it. But at a ball game, you can actually watch a leader as he works to achieve victory. And when the final buzzer sounds or the last out is recorded, you know exactly who won and why. Games have immediate and measurable outcomes.

When I want to see the Law of Victory in action, I go to a game and watch someone such as basketball's Michael Jordan. He is an awesome athlete, but he is also an exceptional leader. He lives and breathes the Law of Victory every day. When the game is on the line, Jordan finds a way for the team to win. His biographer, Mitchell Krugel, says that Jordan's tenacity and passion for victory are evident in every part of his life. He even shows it in practice when the Bulls scrimmage. Krugel explains,

> At Bulls' practices, the starters were known as the white team. The second five wore red. [Former Bulls' coach] Loughery had Jordan playing with the white team from his first day. With Jordan and [teammate] Woolridge, the white team easily rolled up leads of 8-1 or 7-4 in games to 11. The loser of these games always had to run extra wind sprints after practice. It was about that time of the scrimmage that Loughery would switch Jordan to the red team. And the red team would wind up winning more often than not.[5]

Early in his career, Jordan relied heavily on his personal talent and efforts to win games. But as he has matured, he has turned his attention more to being a leader and making the whole team play better. Jordan thinks that many people have overlooked that. He once said, "That's what everybody looks at when I miss a game. Can they win without me? . . . Why doesn't anybody ask why or what it is I contribute that makes a difference? I bet nobody would ever say they miss my leadership or my ability to make my teammates better." Yet that is exactly what he provides. Leaders always find a way for the team to win.

Not long ago Michael Jordan did a commercial for Nike in which he recounted some of his failures: "I've missed over 9,000 shots in my career, lost over 300 games. Twenty-six times I took the game-winning shot and missed." I read an interview with Jordan soon after the commercial first aired where a reporter asked Jordan whether he had really missed that many shots. Jordan's response was revealing: "I have no idea." People may be disappointed by that comment, but it offers insight into his personality. Michael Jordan is not dwelling on his past mistakes. What's important to him is what he can do right now to lead his team to victory.

IT DOESN'T MATTER
WHAT "GAME" THEY'RE IN

There are a lot of great athletes in the game of basketball today. But flashy individual play doesn't always bring victory. What's needed more than anything else is leadership. The greatest players of the past had more than individual talent, though that was definitely present. A player such as Boston center Bill Russell, for example, measured his play by whether it helped the whole team play better. And the result was a remarkable eleven NBA titles. Lakers guard Magic Johnson, who was named NBA Most Valuable Player (MVP) three times and won five championships, was an outstanding scorer, but his greatest contribution was his ability to run the team and get the ball into the hands of his teammates. Larry Bird, who made things happen for the Celtics in the 1980s, is remarkable because he exemplified the Law of Victory not only as a player, but also later as the head coach of the Indiana Pacers. When he was playing in Boston, he was named Rookie of the Year, became the MVP three times, and led his team to three NBA championships. In his first year with the Pacers, he was named NBA Coach of the Year after leading his team to its best-winning percentage in the franchise's history.

Good leaders find a way for their teams to win. That's the Law of Victory. Their particular sport is irrelevant. Michael Jordan, Magic Johnson, and Larry Bird did it in the NBA. John Elway did it in football, leading his team to more fourth-quarter victories than any other quarterback in NFL history. Pelé did it in soccer, winning an unprecedented three World Cups for Brazil. Leaders find a way for the team to succeed.

THREE COMPONENTS OF VICTORY

Whether you're looking at a sports team, an army, a business, or a nonprofit organization, victory is possible as long as you have three components:

1. UNITY OF VISION

Teams succeed only when the players have a unified vision, no matter how much talent or potential there is. A team doesn't win the championship if its players have different agendas. That's true in professional sports. It's true in business. It's true in churches.

I learned this lesson in high school when I was a junior on the varsity basketball team. We had a very talented group of kids, and we had been picked to win the state championship. But we had a problem. The juniors and seniors on the team refused to work together. It got so bad that the coach eventually gave up trying to get us to play together and divided us into two different squads for our games. In the end the team had miserable results. Why? We didn't share a common vision.

> *A team doesn't win the championship if its players have different agendas.*

2. DIVERSITY OF SKILLS

It almost goes without saying that the team needs diversity of skills. Can you imagine a whole hockey team of goalies? Or a football team of quarterbacks? It doesn't make sense. In the same way, organizations require diverse talents to succeed, each player taking his part.

3. A LEADER DEDICATED TO VICTORY AND RAISING PLAYERS TO THEIR POTENTIAL

It's true that having good players with diverse skills is important.

> *"You've got to have great athletes to win, I don't care who the coach is. You can't win without good athletes, but you can lose with them. This is where coaching makes the difference."*
> —*Lou Holtz*

As former Notre Dame head football coach Lou Holtz says, "You've got to have great athletes to win, I don't care who the coach is. You can't win without good athletes, but you can lose with them. This is where coaching makes the difference." In other words, you also require leadership to achieve victory. Unity of vision doesn't happen spontaneously. The right players with the proper diversity of talent don't come together on their own. It takes a leader to make those things happen, and it takes a leader to provide the motivation, empowerment, and direction required to win.

THE LAW OF VICTORY IS HIS BUSINESS

One of the most noteworthy success stories I've come across recently is that of Southwest Airlines and Herb Kelleher, whom I mentioned in the chapter on the Law of Connection. Their story is an admirable example of the Law of Victory in action. Today Southwest looks like a powerhouse that has everything going for it. In the routes where it flies, it dominates the market. The company is on a steady growth curve, and its stock performs extremely well. In fact, it is the only U.S. airline that has earned a profit every year since 1973. Employees love working there. Turnover is extremely low, and the company is considered to have the most productive workforce in the industry. And it's extremely popular with customers; Southwest gets consistently superior customer service ratings.

Given Southwest's current position, you wouldn't suspect that its start-up was anything but smooth. It's a testament to the Law of Victory that the company even exists today. The airline was begun in 1967 by Rollin King, owner of a small commuter air service in Texas; John Parker, a banker; and Herb Kelleher, an attorney. But it took them four years to get their first plane off the ground. As soon as the company incorporated, Braniff, Trans Texas, and Continental Airlines all tried to put it out of business. And they almost succeeded. One court battle followed another, and one man, more than any other, made the fight his own: Herb Kelleher. When their start-up capital was gone, and they seemed to be defeated, the board wanted to give up. However, Kelleher said, "Let's go one more round with them. I will continue to represent the company in court, and I'll postpone any legal fees and pay every cent of the court costs out of my own pocket." Finally when their case made it to the Texas Supreme Court, they won, and they were at last able to put their planes in the air.

Once it got going, Southwest hired experienced airline leader Lamar Muse as its new CEO. He, in turn, hired the best executives available. And as other airlines kept trying to put them out of business, Kelleher and Muse kept fighting—in court and in the marketplace. When they had trouble filling their planes going to and from Houston, Southwest began flying into Houston's Hobby Airport, which was more accessible to commuters because of its proximity to downtown. When all the major carriers moved to the newly created Dallas–Fort Worth Airport, Southwest kept flying into convenient Love Field. When the airline had to sell one of its four planes to survive, the executives figured out a way for their planes to remain on the ground no longer than an amazingly short ten minutes between flights. That way Southwest could maintain routes and schedules. And when they couldn't figure out any other way to fill their planes, they pioneered peak and off-peak pricing, giving leisure travelers a huge break in the cost of fares.

Through it all, Kelleher kept fighting and helped keep Southwest alive. In 1978, seven years after he helped put the company's first small fleet of planes into the air, he became chairman of the company. In 1982, he was made president and CEO. Today he continues to fight and find ways for the company to win. And look at the success:

SOUTHWEST AIRLINES YESTERDAY AND TODAY

	1971	1997
Size of fleet	4	262
Employees at year-end	195	23,974
Customers carried	108,000	50,399,960
Cities served	3	51
Trips flown	6,051	786,288
Stockholders' equity	$3.3 million	$2.0 billion
Total assets	$22 million	$4.2 billion

Southwest's Vice President of Administration Colleen Barrett sums it up: "The warrior mentality, the very fight to survive is truly what created our culture."[6] What Kelleher and Southwest have is not just a will to survive, but a will to win. Leaders who practice the Law of Victory believe that anything less than success is unacceptable. And they have no Plan B. That keeps them fighting.

> *Leaders who practice the Law of Victory have no Plan B. That keeps them fighting.*

What is your level of expectation when it comes to succeeding for your organization? How dedicated are you to winning your "game"? Are you going to have the Law of Victory in your corner as you fight, or when times get difficult, are you going to throw in the towel? Your answer to that question may determine whether you fail or succeed as a leader.

16

THE LAW OF THE BIG MO

Momentum Is a Leader's Best Friend

ALL LEADERS FACE THE challenge of creating change in an organization. The key is momentum—what I call the Big Mo. Just as every sailor knows that you can't steer a ship that isn't moving forward, strong leaders understand that to change direction, you first have to create forward progress—and that takes the Law of the Big Mo.

I saw a movie several years ago called *Stand and Deliver*. Maybe you've seen it too. It's about a real-life teacher named Jaime Escalante who worked at Garfield High School in East Los Angeles, California. The movie focused on Escalante's ability to teach, but the real story is actually a study in the Law of the Big Mo.

Teaching, motivating, and leading were in Jaime Escalante's blood, even from the time of his youth in his native Bolivia. He started tutoring kids when he was in elementary school, and he began his career as a physics teacher before he finished his college degree. He quickly became known as his city's finest teacher. When he was in his thirties, Escalante and his family immigrated to the United

States. He worked several years in a restaurant, and then at Russell Electronics. Though he could have pursued a promising career at Russell, he went back to school and earned a second bachelor's degree so that he could teach in the United States. Escalante's burning desire was to make a difference in people's lives.

At age forty-three, he was hired by Garfield High School to teach computer science. But when he arrived at Garfield on the first day of class, he found that there was no funding for computers. And because his degree was in mathematics, he would be teaching basic math. Disappointed, he went in search of his first class, hoping that his dream of making a difference wasn't slipping through his fingers.

FIGHTING A TIDAL WAVE OF
NEGATIVE MOMENTUM

The change from computers to math turned out to be the least of Escalante's problems. The school, which had been quiet during his summertime interview, was now in chaos. Discipline was nonexistent. Fights seemed to break out continually. Trash and graffiti were everywhere. Students—and even outsiders from the neighborhood—roamed all over the campus throughout the day. Escalante discovered that Alex Avilez, the school's liberal principal, was actually *encouraging* gang recognition on campus. Avilez had decided that student gang members needed validation and more opportunities to identify with the school. So he encouraged eighteen different gangs to put up their *placas* (signs with the gang's symbol) in various places on campus to serve as meeting areas for them. It was a teacher's worst nightmare. How in the world was Escalante going to make a difference under those conditions?

Almost daily he thought of quitting. But his passion for teaching and his dedication to improving the lives of his students wouldn't allow him to give up. Yet at the same time Escalante knew that the students were doomed if the school didn't change. They were all sliding backward fast, and they needed something to move them forward.

The break came as a result of what looked like a major setback: When administrators were informed that the school was in danger of losing its accreditation, the district removed Principal Avilez and replaced him with a better leader, Paul Possemato. He immediately cleaned up the school, discouraged gang activity, and chased outsiders from the campus. Though he was at the school only two years, the principal saved Garfield from losing its accreditation, and he stopped the negative momentum the school had experienced.

IT TAKES A LEADER TO GET THINGS STARTED

The movie *Stand and Deliver* made it look as though Escalante was the one who came up with the idea of preparing students to take an advanced placement (AP) exam. The reality was that a few AP tests were already being given on campus. Each year several students took tests for Spanish. And occasionally, one or two would attempt a test in physics or history. But the problem was that the school didn't have a leader with vision to take up the cause. That's where Escalante came into play. He believed that he and the school could make a positive impact on his students' lives, and the way to start the ball rolling was to challenge the school's best and brightest with an AP calculus test.

SMALL BEGINNINGS

In the fall of 1978, Escalante organized the first calculus class. Rounding up every possible candidate who might be able to handle the course from Garfield's 3,500 student population, he was able to find only fourteen students. In the first few classes, he laid out the work it would take for them to prepare for the AP calculus test at the end of the year.

By the end of the second week of school, he had lost seven students—half the class. Even the ones who stayed were not well prepared for calculus. And by late spring, he was down to only five students. All of them took the AP test in May, but only two passed.

Escalante was disappointed, but he refused to give up, especially since he had made some progress. He knew that if he could give some of the students a few wins, build their confidence, and give them hope, he could move them forward. If he could just build some momentum, things at the school could turn around.

TWO KEYS:
PREPARATION AND MOTIVATION

Escalante recognized that he could succeed only if his students were effectively inspired and properly prepared. Motivation would not be a problem because the calculus teacher was gifted in that area. He read his students masterfully and always knew exactly what to do with them. If they needed motivation, he'd give them extra homework or challenge one of the school's athletes to a handball match. (Escalante never lost!) If they needed encouragement, he'd take them out to McDonald's as a reward. If they got lazy, he'd inspire, amaze, amuse, and even intimidate them. And all along the way, he modeled hard work, dedication to excellence, and what he called *ganas*—desire.

> *Leaders always find a way to make things happen.*

Getting his students prepared was more difficult. He introduced more algebra and trigonometry to students in the lower-level classes, and he got some of his colleagues to do the same. He also started to rally support for a summer program to teach advanced math. And in time, the students improved.

IT STARTS WITH A LITTLE PROGRESS

In the fall, Escalante put together another calculus class, this time with nine students. At the end of the year, eight took the test and six passed. He was making progress. Word of his success spread, and in the fall of 1980, his calculus class numbered fifteen. When they all took the test at the end of the year, fourteen students passed. The steps forward weren't huge, but Escalante could see that the program was building momentum.

The next group of students, numbering eighteen, was the subject of the movie *Stand and Deliver*. Like their predecessors, they worked very hard to learn calculus, many coming to school at 7:00 A.M. every day—a full hour and a half before school started. And often they stayed until 5:00, 6:00, or 7:00 P.M. When they took the test in May, they felt that they had done well.

MOMENTUM BREAKER?

But then there was a problem, one that threatened to destroy the fledgling program and stop cold the momentum Escalante had been working hard to build over the past several years. A grader for the Educational Testing Service (ETS), which administered the AP exams, found some similarities on several of the tests the students had taken. That led to an investigation of fourteen of the eighteen Garfield students who took the test. The testers accused Escalante's students of cheating.

Resolving the investigation was a bureaucratic nightmare. The only way for the students to receive the college credit they wanted so desperately was to retake the test, but the students were indignant and felt retesting was an admission of guilt. Escalante tried to intervene, but the bureaucrats at ETS refused to talk with him. Henry Gradillas, who was then the principal, also tried to get the testing service to reverse its decision but was unsuccessful. They were at an impasse.

Finally, the students agreed to retake the test—even though they had been out of school and hadn't studied for three months. What were the results? Every single student passed. Escalante's pass rate for the year was 100 percent.

NO—MOMENTUM MAKER

What could have killed the momentum Escalante had built at Garfield turned into a real momentum builder. Students at the school became more confident, and people within the community rallied around Escalante and his program. And the publicity surrounding the test gave a push of momentum that made it possible for East Los Angeles College to start a summer program that Escalante wanted for his students.

After that, the math program exploded. In 1983, the number of students passing the AP calculus exam almost doubled, from 18 to 31. The next year it doubled again, the number reaching 63. And it continued growing. In 1987, 129 students took the test, with 85 of them receiving college credit. Garfield High School in East Los Angeles, once considered the sinkhole of the district, produced 27 percent of all passing AP calculus test scores by Mexican-Americans in the entire United States.

THE MOMENTUM EXPLOSION

The benefits of the Law of the Big Mo were felt by all of Garfield High School's students. The school started offering classes to prepare students for other AP exams. In time, Garfield held regular AP classes in Spanish, calculus, history, European history, biology, physics, French, government, and computer science.

In 1987, nine years after Escalante spearheaded the program, Garfield students took more than 325 AP examinations. Most incredibly, Garfield had a waiting list of more than four hundred students from areas outside its boundaries wanting to enroll. The school that was once the laughingstock of the district and that had almost lost its accreditation had become one of the top three inner-city schools in the entire nation![1] That's the power of the Law of the Big Mo.

ONLY A LEADER CAN CREATE MOMENTUM

It takes a leader to create momentum. Followers catch it. And managers are able to continue it once it has begun. But *creating* it requires someone who can motivate others, not who needs to be motivated. Harry Truman once said, "If you can't stand the heat, get out

> *If you can't* make *some heat, get out of the kitchen.*

of the kitchen." But for leaders, that statement should be changed to read, "If you can't *make* some heat, get out of the kitchen."

TRUTHS ABOUT MOMENTUM

Momentum really is a leader's best friend. Sometimes it's the only difference between losing and winning. That's why in basketball games, for instance, when the opposing team scores a lot of unanswered points and starts to develop too much momentum, a good coach will call a time-out. He knows that if the other team's momentum gets too strong, his team is likely to lose the game.

Momentum also makes a huge difference in organizations. When you have no momentum, even the simplest tasks can seem to be insurmountable problems. But when you have momentum on your side, the future looks bright, obstacles appear small, and trouble seems temporary.

MOMENTUM MAKES LEADERS LOOK BETTER
THAN THEY ARE

When leaders have momentum on their side, people think they're geniuses. They look past shortcomings. They forget about the mistakes the leaders have made. Momentum changes people's perspective of leaders.

MOMENTUM HELPS FOLLOWERS PERFORM BETTER
THAN THEY ARE

When leadership is strong and there is momentum in an organization, people are motivated and inspired to perform at higher levels. They become effective beyond their hopes and expectations.

> *With enough momentum, nearly any kind of change is possible.*

If you remember the 1980 U.S. Olympic hockey team, you know what I'm talking about. The team was good, but not good enough to win the gold medal. Yet that's what the Americans did. Why? Because leading up to the championship game, they won game after game against very tough teams. They gained so much momentum that they performed beyond their capabilities. And after they beat the Russians, nothing could stop them from coming home with the gold medal.

MOMENTUM IS EASIER TO STEER THAN TO START

Have you ever been waterskiing? If you have, you know that it's harder to get up on the water than it is to steer once you're up there. Think about the first time you skied. Before you got up, the boat was dragging you along, and you probably thought your arms were going to give way as the water flooded against your chest and into your face. For a moment, you might have believed you couldn't hold on to the tow rope any longer. But then the force of the water drove your skis up onto the surface, and off you went. At that point, you were able to make a turn with only a subtle shift of weight from one foot to another. That's the way the momentum of leadership works. Getting started is a struggle, but once you're moving forward, you can really start to do some amazing things.

MOMENTUM IS THE MOST POWERFUL CHANGE AGENT

With enough momentum, nearly any kind of change is possible. That was true for Garfield High School, considered by many people to be a place with no hope, and it's true for any other organization. Momentum puts victory within reach.

MY GREATEST MOMENTUM CHALLENGE

As a leader, my greatest fight for momentum occurred at Skyline, my third church. I arrived there as the senior pastor in 1981, and as the church started growing, it didn't take me long to recognize that we would need to relocate to sustain our growth.

At first, I thought that wouldn't be a problem. A relocation that size isn't easy, but we were in a good position for the move. We had started to develop momentum, having doubled in size from one thousand to more than two thousand in attendance. Through my application of the Law of the Inner Circle, we had an exceptional staff in place. Morale among the people was very high. And I also had the advantage of having led both of my previous churches through building projects. But I failed to take into account the depth of San Diego's bureaucracy and California's environmental protection laws.

When I was the pastor at my first church in Indiana, we had gone through a rapid period of growth and decided to relocate. After the decision was made to construct a new building, a member of the church donated a plot of land, and we started building within a few weeks. In less than nine months, we had built a new facility and moved in.

Things couldn't have been more different in California. We started the relocation process in 1984. Because of local politics, neighborhood concerns, and environmental red tape, what appeared to be a three-year project dragged out for more than three times that long. As it turned out, it took us eleven years *just to get the zoning and building permits approved.* I wasn't the leader anymore when the project finally received approval. Jim Garlow, who followed me as the senior pastor at the church, accomplished that along with a fine team of laypeople.

The greatest challenge of my life as a leader was sustaining momentum during those last five years at Skyline. The people at most churches facing similar circumstances would have given up, and before long, their churches would have shrunk in size. But not Skyline. What saved us? The answer can be found in the Law of the Big Mo. I did everything possible during those years to build momentum. I continually kept the vision for the relocation in front of the people. We made it a habit to focus on what we *could* do rather than on what we couldn't, and we often celebrated our victories, no matter how small. Meanwhile, we made progress in areas where we could. We improved our small groups, making them very strong, and we continually focused on developing leaders. It kept us going. The momentum we built was so strong that even that eleven-year obstacle couldn't stop us.

If your desire is to do great things with your organization, never overlook the power of momentum. It truly is the leader's best friend. If you can develop it, you can do almost anything. That's the power of the Big Mo.

17

THE LAW OF PRIORITIES

*Leaders Understand That Activity Is
Not Necessarily Accomplishment*

L EADERS NEVER GROW to a point where they no longer need to prioritize. It's something that good leaders keep doing, whether they're leading a small group, pastoring a church, running a small business, or leading a billion-dollar corporation. I was reminded of that last year when I moved my companies from San Diego, California, to Atlanta, Georgia.

I used to think that I would live the rest of my life in San Diego. It's a gorgeous city with one of the best climates in the world. It's ten minutes from the beach and two hours from the ski slopes. It has culture, professional sporting teams, and fine restaurants. And I could play golf there year-round. Why would I ever want to leave a place like that?

> *"A leader
> is the one who
> climbs the tallest
> tree, surveys the
> entire situation,
> and yells,
> 'Wrong jungle!'"*
> —Stephen Covey

But then one day I sat down and started to reevaluate my priorities. I fly a tremendous amount because of my speaking engagements and consulting work. I realized that because I lived in San Diego, I was spending too much time traveling just to various airline hubs in order to make connections. So I asked Linda, my assistant, to figure out exactly how much time I was doing that. What I discovered shocked even me. In 1996, I had spent twenty-seven *days* traveling back and forth just between San Diego and Dallas to make flight connections. That's when I decided to look into moving INJOY and my other companies to an airline hub. Stephen Covey remarked, "A leader is the one who climbs the tallest tree, surveys the entire situation, and yells, 'Wrong jungle!'" I felt a little like that when I realized what we were about to do.

We finally settled on Atlanta as the ideal location. First, it was a major airline hub. From there I would be able to reach 80 percent of the United States with a two-hour flight. That would give me a lot of extra time in the coming years. Second, the area is beautiful, and it offers excellent cultural, recreational, and entertainment opportunities. Finally, my people moving from California would be able to enjoy a good standard of living. The move was quite an undertaking, but it went smoothly thanks to the hard work and strong leadership of the people who work for me.

THE THREE Rs

Immediately after our move to Atlanta, I also set aside some time to reevaluate my personal priorities. For the last several years, my schedule has gotten heavier and heavier. And the size of our organizations has grown. Four years ago, we had fewer than twenty employees. Now we have more than one hundred. But just because we're doing more doesn't automatically mean that we're being successful and accomplishing our mission. For that, you have to look to the Law of Priorities.

For the last ten years, I've used two guidelines to help me measure my activity and determine my priorities. The first is the Pareto

Principle. I've often taught it to people at leadership conferences over the years, and I also explain it in my book *Developing the Leader Within You*. The idea is this: If you focus your attention on the activities that rank in the top 20 percent in terms of importance, you will have an 80 percent return on your effort. For example, if you have ten employees, you should give 80 percent of your time and attention to your best two people. If you have one hundred customers, the top twenty will provide you with 80 percent of your business. If your to-do list has

> *"There are many things that will catch my eye, but there are only a few things that will catch my heart."*
> —*Tim Redmond*

ten items on it, the two most important ones will give you an 80 percent return on your time. If you haven't already observed this phenomenon, test it and you'll see that it really works out.

The second guideline is the three Rs. No, they're not reading, writing, and 'rithmetic. My three Rs are requirement, return, and reward. To be effective, leaders must order their lives according to these three questions:

1. WHAT IS REQUIRED?

We're all accountable to somebody—an employer, a board of directors, our stockholders, or someone else. For that reason, your list of priorities must always begin with what is required of you. Anything required that's not necessary for you to do personally should be delegated or eliminated.

2. WHAT GIVES THE GREATEST RETURN?

As a leader, you should spend most of your time working in your areas of greatest strength. If something can be done 80 percent as well by someone else in your organization, delegate it. If a responsibility could *potentially* meet that standard, then develop a person to handle it.

3. WHAT BRINGS THE GREATEST REWARD?

Tim Redmond admitted, "There are many things that will catch my eye, but there are only a few things that will catch my heart." The things that bring the greatest personal reward are the fire lighters in a leader's life. Nothing energizes a person the way passion does.

REORDERING PRIORITIES

My most important priority after the move to Atlanta was to carve out more time for my family. So I discussed that issue with my wife, Margaret, and we came to an agreement concerning what our time would look like. Then I brought together the four presidents of my organizations and several other key players to help me review my other priorities and determine how I would spend my time in the coming year. As we talked through the issues, they shared their needs with me, and I shared my vision with them. Together, we confirmed the amount of time I would give each of my four key priority areas. Here's what we came up with:

AREA	TIME ALLOTTED
1. Leadership	19 percent
2. Communicating	38 percent
3. Creating	31 percent
4. Networking	12 percent

I am passionate about each of these four areas. All of them are absolutely necessary for the growth and health of the organizations, and they bring the highest return for my time. So far these guidelines seem to be serving the companies and me well. But every year we will revisit them and take a hard look at how effective we're being. Activity is not necessarily accomplishment. If we want to continue to be effective, we have to work according to the Law of Priorities.

PRIORITIES WERE THE
NAME OF HIS GAME

Examine the life of any great leader, and you will see him putting priorities into action. Every time Norman Schwarzkopf assumed a new command, he didn't just rely on his leadership intuition; he also reexamined the unit's priorities. When Lee Iacocca took over Chrysler, the first thing he did was to reorder its priorities. When explorer Roald Amundsen succeeded in taking his team to the South Pole and back, it was due, in part, to his ability to set right priorities.

Successful leaders live according to the Law of Priorities. They recognize that activity is not necessarily accomplishment. But the best leaders seem to be able to get the Law of Priorities to work for them by satisfying multiple priorities with each activity. This actually enables them to increase their focus while reducing their number of actions.

A leader who was a master at that was one of my idols: John Wooden, the former head basketball coach of the UCLA Bruins. He is called the Wizard of Westwood because the amazing feats he accomplished in the world of college sports were so incredible that they seemed to be magical.

Evidence of Wooden's ability to make the Law of Priorities work for him could be seen in the way he approached basketball practice. Wooden claimed that he learned some of his methods from watching Frank Leahy, the great former Notre Dame football head coach. He said, "I often went to his [Leahy's] practices and observed how he broke them up into periods. Then I would go home and analyze why he did things certain ways. As a player, I realized there was a great deal of time wasted. Leahy's concepts reinforced my ideas and helped in the ultimate development of what I do now."

EVERYTHING HAD A PURPOSE
BASED ON PRIORITIES

Friends who have been in the military tell me that they often had to hurry up and wait. That seems to be the way some coaches work too. Their players are asked to work their hearts out one minute and then to stand around doing nothing the next. But that's not the way Wooden worked. He orchestrated every moment of practice and planned each activity with specific purposes in mind.

Every year, Wooden determined a list of overall priorities for the team, based on observations from the previous season. Those items might include objectives such as, "Build confidence in Drollinger and Irgovich," or "Use 3 on 2 continuity drill at least three times a week." Usually, he had about a dozen or so items that he wanted to work on throughout the season. But Wooden also reviewed his agenda for his teams every day. Each morning, he and an assistant would meticulously plan the day's practice. They usually spent two hours strategizing for a practice that might not even last that long. He drew ideas from notes jotted on three-by-five cards that he always carried with him. He planned every drill, minute by minute, and recorded the information in a notebook prior to practice. Wooden once boasted that if you asked what his team was doing on a specific date at three o'clock in 1963, he could tell you precisely what drill his team was running.

Wooden always maintained his focus, and he found ways for his players to do the same thing. His special talent was for addressing several priority areas at once. For example, to help players work on their free throws—something that many of them found tedious— Wooden instituted a free-throw shooting policy during scrimmages that would encourage them to concentrate and improve instead of just marking time. The sooner a sidelined player made a set number of shots, the sooner he could get back into action. And Wooden continually changed the number of shots required by the guards, forwards, and centers so that team members rotated in and out at different rates. That way everyone, regardless of position or starting status, got experience playing, a critical priority for Wooden's development of total teamwork.

The most remarkable aspect about John Wooden—and the most telling about his ability to focus on his priorities—is that he never scouted opposing teams. Instead, he focused on getting his players to reach *their* potential. And he addressed those things through practice and personal interaction with the players. It was never his goal to win championships or even to beat the other team. His desire was to get each person to play to his potential and to put the best possible team on the floor. And of course, Wooden's results were incredible. In more than forty years of coaching, he had only *one* losing season—his first. And he led his UCLA teams to four undefeated seasons and a record ten NCAA championships.[1] No other college team has ever come close. Wooden is a great leader. He just might be the finest man to coach in any sport. Why? Because every day he lived by the Law of Priorities.

REFOCUSING ON A WORLDWIDE SCALE

One of the most effective leaders today when it comes to the Law of Priorities is Jack Welch, chairman and CEO of General Electric, whom I mentioned in discussing the Law of Reproduction. When Welch assumed leadership of GE in 1981, it was a good company. It had a ninety-year history, the company stock traded at $4 per share, and the company was worth about $12 billion, eleventh best on the stock market. It was a huge, diverse company that included 350 strategic businesses. But Welch believed the company could become better. What was his strategy? He used the Law of Priorities.

Within a few months of taking over the company, he began what he called the hardware revolution. It changed the entire profile and focus of the company. Welch said,

> To the hundreds of businesses and product lines that made up the company we applied a single criterion: can they be number 1 or number 2 at whatever they do in the world marketplace? Of the 348 businesses or product lines that could not, we closed some and divested others. Their sale brought in almost $10 billion. We invested $18 billion in the ones that remained and further strengthened them with $17 billion worth of acquisitions.
>
> What remained [in 1989], aside from a few relatively small supporting operations, are 14 world-class businesses . . . all well positioned for the '90s . . . each one either first or second in the world market in which it participates.[2]

Welch's strong leadership and ability to focus have paid incredible dividends. Since he took over, GE's stock has experienced a 2 to 1 split four times. And it trades at more than $80 per share as I write this. The company is currently ranked as the nation's most admired company according to *Fortune,* and it has recently become the most valuable company in the world, with a market capitalization of more than $250 billion.

What has made GE one of the best companies in the world? Jack Welch's ability to use the Law of Priorities in his leadership. He never mistook activity for accomplishment. He knew that the greatest success comes only when you focus your people on what really matters.

Take some time to reassess your leadership priorities. Like GE in the early '80s, are you spread out all over the place? Or are you focused on the few things that bring the highest reward? If you aren't living by the Law of Priorities, you might be spinning your wheels.

18

THE LAW OF SACRIFICE

A Leader Must Give Up to Go Up

O NE OF THE MOST incredible turnarounds in American business history dramatically demonstrates the Law of Sacrifice. It happened at the Chrysler Corporation in the early 1980s. Chrysler was in a mess, despite a prior history of success. The company has been around since the mid-1920s, when Walter Chrysler reorganized the Maxwell and Chalmers Motor Car Companies and gave the business his name. In 1928, he bought out Dodge and Plymouth, and by 1940, the year he died, he had the second largest auto company in the world, ahead of Ford, the pioneer of the industry, and behind only General Motors. It was a tremendous success story. At one point, Chrysler had captured 25 percent of the entire domestic automobile market.

The company remained fairly strong through the 1960s. A hallmark of its cars was innovative engineering. For example, Chrysler engineers designed the first electronic ignition for cars, the first hydraulic brakes, and the first under-the-hood computer. And in the 1960s, its cars were also known for high performance, with models such as the Barracuda, the Dodge Daytona, and the Plymouth Road Runner—called by some the ultimate street racer.

A DEVASTATING DOWNTURN

But by the 1970s, the company was declining rapidly. In 1978, its market share was down from 25 percent to a puny 11 percent. And things were getting worse. The organization was headed for bankruptcy. Then in November 1978, Chrysler brought aboard a new leader. His name was Lee Iacocca. He was a seasoned car man who had worked his way up through the ranks at Ford. Though educated as an engineer, he had voluntarily started his career in sales for Ford in Pennsylvania in the 1940s and eventually earned his way to headquarters in Dearborn, Michigan. While there, he led teams who created groundbreaking automobiles such as the Lincoln Continental Mark III and the legendary Mustang, one of the most popular cars in history.

In 1970, Iacocca became the president of the Ford Motor Company, the highest leadership position possible under Chairman Henry Ford II. In all, Iacocca worked for Ford for thirty-two years. And when he left in 1978, the company was earning record profits, having made $1.8 billion in *each* of his last two years running the business. Though the separation wasn't pleasant, between the severance package he received and the stock he had acquired while at Ford, Iacocca was in a position where he would never have to work again. But he was only fifty-four years old when he left Ford, and he knew he still had a lot to offer an organization.

LEADER TO THE RESCUE

Chrysler's invitation for him to come on board presented him with the opportunity—and the challenge—of a lifetime. John Riccardo, then chairman of the board for Chrysler, recognized that the company needed strong leadership to survive, something he could not adequately provide. According to Iacocca, Riccardo knew that he was in over his head, so he wanted to bring in the former Ford man as president of Chrysler. In turn, Riccardo would step aside in less than two years so that Iacocca could become chairman and CEO. John Riccardo was willing to sacrifice himself for the good of the company. As a result, Iacocca would have the chance to realize a lifelong dream: becoming the top man at one of the Big Three.

IACOCCA GAVE UP TO GO UP

Iacocca accepted the job, but it also started him down his own road of personal sacrifice. The first came in his finances. The salary he accepted at Chrysler was a little over half of what he had earned as the president of Ford. The next sacrifice came in his family life. At Ford, Iacocca had always prided himself on the fact that he worked hard from Monday to Friday, but he always set aside Saturday, Sunday, and most Friday nights for his family. And when he came home from work at the end of the day, he left his troubles at the office.

> *The Law of Sacrifice says you have to give up to go up.*

But to lead Chrysler, he had to work almost around the clock. On top of that, when he got home, he couldn't sleep. Iacocca later described the company as having been run like a small grocery store, despite its size. There were no viable financial systems or controls in place, production and supply methods were a mess, products were poorly built, and nearly all of the divisions were run by turf-minded vice presidents who refused to work as a team. Morale was abysmal throughout the company, customer loyalty was the worst in the business, and the company continued to lose money.

WHEN ALL ELSE FAILS,
MAKE ANOTHER SACRIFICE

Iacocca understood that successful leaders have to maintain an attitude of sacrifice in order to turn around an organization. They have
to be willing to do what it takes to go to the next level. Iacocca fired
thirty-three of the thirty-five vice presidents during a three-year
period. Yet things continued to worsen. The country was experiencing a terrible recession, and interest rates were the highest they had
ever been. Then oil prices skyrocketed when the shah of Iran was
deposed in early 1979. Chrysler's market
share fell to a weak 8 percent. Despite all
Iacocca's work, it seemed as if the Law of
Sacrifice wasn't working.

> *The Law
> of Sacrifice
> maintains that
> one sacrifice
> seldom brings
> success.*

Iacocca worked harder to rebuild the company by bringing in the very best leaders in
the business, many of whom had retired from
Ford. He cut every expense he could and built
on the company's strengths, but those measures weren't enough to lift
up the company. Chrysler was headed for bankruptcy. Iacocca had to
face the greatest personal sacrifice of all: He would go to the
American government with his proverbial hat in his hand for loan
guarantees.

At Ford, Iacocca had developed a reputation for being highly critical of any government involvement in business. So when he
approached Congress for help, no one spoke very kindly about him.
Iacocca later discussed that episode:

In the minds of Congress and the media, we had sinned. We had
missed the market, and we deserved to be punished.

And punished we were. During the congressional hearings,
we were held up before the entire world as living examples of

everything that was wrong with American industry. We were humiliated on the editorial pages for not having the decency to give up and die gracefully . . . Our wives and kids were the butt of jokes in shopping malls and schools. It was a far higher price to pay than just closing the doors and walking away. It was personal. It was pointed. And it was painful.

Swallowing his pride was a heroic sacrifice for Iacocca, one that many top corporate executives never would have made. But it was a price he had to pay to save the company.

At least one sacrifice he made at that time received positive press: Iacocca reduced his own salary to one dollar a year. At the time he said, "Leadership means setting an example. When you find yourself in a position of leadership, people follow your every move." He followed that action with requests for others to make sacrifices. He asked Chrysler's top executives to take a 10 percent pay cut. Then he asked for—and received—concessions from the unions and the banks that were working with the automaker. For Chrysler to succeed, they would all make sacrifices together. And succeed they did. By 1982, Chrysler generated an operating profit of $925 million, the best in its history. And in 1983, the company was able to repay its loans.[1]

> "Leadership means setting an example. When you find yourself in a position of leadership, people follow your every move."
> —Lee Iacocca

Chrysler has continued to succeed and grow. The company has fought its way back, and today it has a combined U.S. and Canadian market share of more than 16 percent—double what it was in the early years when Iacocca took over. He has since retired, but his leadership put Chrysler back on the map. Why? Because he modeled the Law of Sacrifice.

THE HEART OF LEADERSHIP

What was true for Lee Iacocca is true for any leader. You have to give up to go up. Many people today want to climb up the corporate ladder because they believe that freedom and power are the prizes waiting at the top. They don't realize that the true nature of leadership is really sacrifice.

Most people will acknowledge that sacrifices are necessary fairly early in a leadership career. People give up many things in order to gain potential opportunities. For example, Tom Murphy began working for General Motors in 1937. But he almost refused the first position he was offered with the company because the one-hundred-dollars-a-month salary barely covered his expenses. Despite his misgivings, he took the job anyway, thinking the opportunity was worth the sacrifice. He was right. Murphy eventually became General Motors' chairman of the board.

COUNTING THE COST OF LEADERSHIP

Sacrifice is a constant in leadership. It is an ongoing process, not a one-time payment. When I look back at my career, I recognize that there has always been a cost involved in moving forward. That's been true for me in the area of finances with every career change I've made except one. When I accepted my first job, our family income decreased since my position paid little and my wife, Margaret, had to give up her job as a schoolteacher for me to take it. When I accepted a director's job at denominational headquarters in Marion, Indiana, I once again took a pay cut. After I interviewed for my third pastoral position, I accepted the position from the board without knowing what the

> *Sacrifice is an ongoing process, not a one-time payment.*

salary would be. (It was lower.) When some board members expressed their surprise, I told them that if I did the job well, the salary would take care of itself. And in 1995 when I finally left the church after a twenty-six-year career so that I could teach leadership full-time, I gave up a salary altogether. Anytime you know that the step is right, don't hesitate to make a sacrifice.

YOU'VE GOT TO GIVE UP TO GO UP

Leaders who want to rise have to do more than take an occasional cut in pay. They have to give up their rights. As my friend Gerald Brooks says, "When you become a leader, you lose the right to think about yourself." For every person, the nature of the sacrifice may be different. For example, Iacocca's greatest sacrifices came late in his career. In the case of someone like former South African president F. W. de Klerk, who worked to dismantle apartheid in his country, the cost was his career itself. The

> *"When you become a leader, you lose the right to think about yourself."*
> —*Gerald Brooks*

circumstances may change from person to person, but the principle doesn't. Leadership means sacrifice.

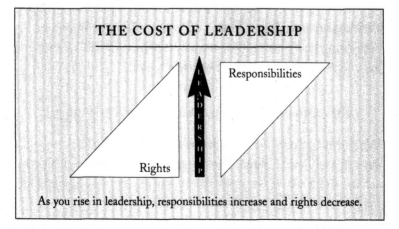

THE COST OF LEADERSHIP

Responsibilities

Rights

LEADERSHIP

As you rise in leadership, responsibilities increase and rights decrease.

Leaders give up to go up. That's true of every leader regardless of profession. Talk to any leader, and you will find that he has made repeated sacrifices. Usually, the higher that leader has climbed, the greater the sacrifices he has made. Effective leaders sacrifice much that is good in order to dedicate themselves to what is best. That's the way the Law of Sacrifice works. Digital Chairman and Chief Executive Robert Palmer said in an interview, "In my model of management, there's very little wiggle room. If you want a management job, then you have to accept the responsibility and accountability that goes with it."[2] He is really talking about the cost of leadership.

If leaders have to give up to go up, then they have to give up even more to stay up. Have you ever considered how infrequently teams have back-to-back championship seasons? The reason is simple: If a leader can take a team to the championship game and win it, he often assumes he can duplicate the results the next year without making changes. He becomes reluctant to make additional sacrifices in the off-season. But what gets a team to the top isn't what keeps it there. The only way to stay up is to give up even more. Leadership success requires continual change, improvement, and sacrifice.

> *If leaders have to give up to go up, then they have to give up even more to stay up.*

Philosopher-poet Ralph Waldo Emerson offered this option: "For everything you have missed, you have gained something else; and for everything you gain, you lose something."

THE HIGHER YOU GO, THE MORE YOU GIVE UP

Who is the most powerful leader in the world? I'd say it's the president of the United States. More than any other single person, his actions and words make an impact on people, not just in our country, but around the globe. Think about what he must give up to reach the office of president and then to hold that office. His time is no longer his own. He is scrutinized constantly. His family is under tremendous pressure. And as a matter of course, he must make decisions that can cost thousands of people their lives. Even after he leaves office, he will spend the rest of his life in the company of Secret Service agents who protect him from bodily harm.

> *"For everything you have missed, you have gained something else; and for everything you gain, you lose something."*
> —*Ralph Waldo Emerson*

The Law of Sacrifice demands that the greater the leader, the more he must give up. Think about someone like Martin Luther King Jr. His wife, Coretta Scott King, remarked in *My Life with Martin Luther King, Jr.*, "Day and night our phone would ring, and someone would pour out a string of obscene epithets . . . Frequently the calls ended with a threat to kill us if we didn't get out of town. But in spite of all the danger, the chaos of our private lives, I felt inspired, almost elated."

While pursuing his course of leadership during the civil rights movement, King was arrested and jailed on many occasions. He was stoned, stabbed, and physically attacked. His house was bombed. Yet his vision—and his influence—continued to increase. Ultimately, he sacrificed everything he had. But what he gave up he parted with willingly. In his last speech, delivered the night before his assassination in Memphis, he said,

> I don't know what will happen to me now. We've got some difficult days ahead. But it doesn't matter to me now. Because I've been to the mountaintop. I won't mind. Like anybody else, I would like to live a long life. Longevity has its place. But I'm not concerned about that now. I just want to do God's will. And He's allowed me to go up to the mountain. And I've looked over and

I've seen the Promised Land. I may not get there with you, but I want you to know tonight that we, as a people, will get to the Promised Land. So I'm happy tonight . . . I'm not fearing any man. "Mine eyes have seen the glory of the coming of the Lord."[3]

The next day he paid the ultimate price of sacrifice. King's impact was profound. He influenced millions of people to peacefully stand up against a system and society that fought to exclude them.

> *The higher the level of leadership people want to reach, the greater the sacrifices they will have to make.*

What successful people find to be true becomes even clearer to them when they become leaders. There is no success without sacrifice. The higher the level of leadership you want to reach, the greater the sacrifices you will have to make. To go up, you have to give up. That is the true nature of leadership. That is the Law of Sacrifice.

THE LAW OF TIMING

When to Lead Is As Important As
What to Do and Where to Go

Tʜᴇ ʟᴀᴡ ᴏꜰ ᴛɪᴍɪɴɢ gave him the chance to become president of the United States. It was a volatile time in the nation's history. Everyone was worn out from the war in Vietnam and the disgrace of Watergate. The people were discouraged and demoralized. And they were especially skeptical of anyone who had *any* connection with Washington government. While campaigning for office, this future president, who had never served in Washington, said about himself, "I have been accused of being an outsider. I plead guilty. Unfortunately, the vast majority of Americans . . . are also outsiders."[1] That person was Jimmy Carter.

THE TIMING WAS RIGHT FOR AN OUTSIDER

When you understand the Law of Timing, you see why Jimmy Carter was elected president of the United States in 1976. In fact, Carter's life and career are characterized by one well-timed move after another. A graduate of Annapolis, Carter had intended to spend his career in the U.S. Navy, but when his father unexpectedly died in 1953, he returned to Plains, Georgia, to take over the family business. In only a few years, he became a strong, respected businessman and a leader in the community.

In 1962, times were changing. The old political machine in Georgia with its corrupt methods of electing officials was beginning to crumble, and Carter decided to run for the Georgia senate. Carter recognized that for the first time in history, a person who was not part of the old system had a chance of being elected to office. But he faced a huge battle. The entrenched political bosses were still fighting to maintain control of their turf. One corrupt leader openly intimidated voters in his district and falsified voting records. As a result, Carter lost the primary. But he refused to quit without a battle. He fought the results of the primary and appealed to a superior court judge to have the voting process reviewed. When the results were overturned, Carter was able to stay on the ticket, and he went on to win the election. Then in 1970, he successfully ran for governor. Once again, he recognized that the timing was right for a relative newcomer to challenge the established political machine.

NONLEADERS CAN'T ALWAYS SEE IT

What Carter did next was almost unthinkable. He decided to run for president of the United States. Here was a man whose entire career as an elected politician consisted of one term in the Georgia senate and one term as the state's governor. His experience was minimal, and he had no presence on the national scene. Carter was such an unknown that when he appeared on the television show *What's My Line?* in 1973 while governor, the panelists didn't know him and couldn't guess his profession.

When Carter first threw his hat into the ring for the presidency, people in the media ignored him. They figured that a little-known ex-governor from the South with no Washington experience had no kind of chance to obtain the Democratic nomination, much less achieve the presidency. But Carter was undaunted. He and a few key associates had recognized that the timing would be right for him in 1976, and they met to talk about it. Carter biographer Peter G. Bourne, who attended the meeting, said that he saw "a unique, open opportunity for an outsider to run for the presidency." Carter saw it, too; he knew that it was a now-or-never proposition.

Carter made his candidacy for president official in December of 1975, a year after finishing his term as governor. The reaction of people across the nation was painfully indifferent. Bourne reported,

> Most journalists seemed not to grasp the profound social and political currents affecting the country. The impact of Vietnam, Watergate, the change in race relations in the South, and especially the profound opening up of the political process seemed largely ignored, and candidates were examined only within the context of the old political paradigm.[2]

The Law of Timing showed that it was the right time for an outsider to run, and Carter was everything that recent presidents had not been: He held no public office while campaigning, having finished his term as governor in 1974. He was not a lawyer by profession. He was a vocal proponent of his Christian faith. And unlike the people who had previously held the nation's highest office, he had not been a part of Washington politics as a congressman, senator, vice president, or cabinet member. His was a fresh face with a different approach to government, something the American people desperately wanted. I believe that at no other time—either before or since—would Jimmy Carter have been elected. Remarkably, on January 20, 1977, James Earl Carter was inaugurated as thirty-ninth president of the United States.

However, timing was not always Jimmy Carter's friend. When the 1980 election rolled around, it killed his chances for reelection. The country was experiencing as many problems as it ever had. The economy was a mess: Americans faced double-digit inflation, record-high oil prices, and skyrocketing mortgage rates. There were also numerous foreign policy problems, including the Soviet invasion of Afghanistan and, of course, the long captivity of the American hostages in Iran. A botched rescue attempt to free the captives further worked against Carter. After the returns came in on the night of the election, Carter found that he had won only an abysmal 49 electoral votes to Ronald Reagan's 489. It was a devastating defeat. The Law of Timing is a double-edged sword. Just as it served to elect Carter president in 1976, it worked against him four years later.

TIMING IS EVERYTHING

Great leaders recognize that *when* to lead is as important as what to do and where to go. Every time a leader makes a move, there are really only four outcomes that can result:

1. THE WRONG ACTION AT THE WRONG TIME
LEADS TO DISASTER

A leader who takes the wrong action at the wrong time is sure to suffer negative repercussions. When U.S. forces attempted to rescue the Iranian-held hostages during the Carter administration, it was an example of the wrong action at the wrong time. Prior to the decision to try the rescue, Secretary of State Cyrus Vance had argued that the plan was flawed. He believed something would go wrong. Unfortunately, he was right. Several helicopters experienced mechanical problems, one got lost in a sandstorm, and another crashed into a transport plane, killing eight servicemen. Peter

Bourne described it as "a combination of bad luck and military ineptitude." It could be described only as a disaster. It was an exercise in bad timing, and as much as anything else, it signaled the end of Carter's chances to be reelected.

2. THE RIGHT ACTION AT THE WRONG TIME BRINGS RESISTANCE

It's one thing to figure out *what* needs to be done; it's another to understand *when* to make a move. I remember an example of this kind of bad timing from my leadership experience. In the early 1980s, I tried to start a small group program at Skyline, my church in San Diego. It was the right thing to do, but it failed miserably. Why? The timing was

> *If a leader repeatedly shows poor judgment, even in little things, people start to think that having him as the leader is the real mistake.*

wrong. We hadn't recognized that we had developed too few leaders to support the launch. But six years later, when we tried again, the program was very successful. It was all a matter of timing.

3. THE WRONG ACTION AT THE RIGHT TIME IS A MISTAKE

For about a decade, various colleagues of mine tried to talk me into doing a radio program. For a long time I resisted the idea. But a couple of years ago, I recognized that the time was right. So we created a program called *Growing Today*. However, there was one problem: the format. I wanted to get materials into the hands of people to help them, but I was determined not to accept donations from the public. The solution, I thought, was to air a growth-oriented program and depend on product sales to support it. We found out that it was a mistake. That type of show could not break even. Radio was right, but the type of show was wrong. The Law of Timing had spoken again.

4. THE RIGHT ACTION AT THE RIGHT TIME RESULTS IN SUCCESS

When leaders do the right things at the right time, success is almost inevitable. People, principles, and processes converge to make an incredible impact. And the results touch not only the leader but also the followers and the whole organization.

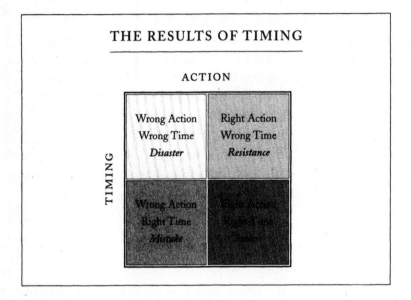

When the right leader and the right timing come together, incredible things happen. Think about the life of Winston Churchill.

> When the right leader and the right timing come together, incredible things happen.

It wasn't until he was in his sixties that he became prime minister of England. A soldier, writer, and statesman, he had spent his life leading others, but only during the Second World War was the timing right for him to emerge as a great leader. And once the war was over, the people who had rallied around him dismissed him.

During his eightieth birthday address to Parliament on November 30, 1954, Churchill reflected on his role in Great Britain's leadership: "I have never accepted what many people have kindly said—namely that I inspired the nation. Their will was resolute and remorseless, and as it proved, unconquerable. It fell to me to express it. It was the nation and the race dwelling all round the globe that had the lion's heart. I had the luck to be called upon to give the roar."[3]

Churchill's contribution really had nothing to do with luck, but it had a lot to do with timing. He understood the impact that timing can have on a person's life. Another time he described it like this: "There comes a special moment in everyone's life, a moment for which that person was born. That special opportunity, when he seizes it, will fulfill his mission—a mission for which he is uniquely qualified. In that moment, he finds greatness. It is his finest hour."

THE CRUCIBLE OF WAR
DISPLAYS THE LAW OF TIMING

Churchill's experience shows that the Law of Timing becomes especially obvious during times of war. You could see it at work in the 1991 Gulf War with Iraq. In the early stages of Desert Shield, the big concern was to get enough troops and equipment into place to effectively defend Saudi Arabia. If Iraq attacked before the defenders arrived, another country would be lost to Saddam Hussein's aggression.

Then the goal was to deploy enough forces to win decisively against the Iraqis. The coalition forces bided their time and waged a successful air campaign before launching Desert Storm to push Iraq out of Kuwait. And the proof of their good timing can be seen in the results: While Iraq suffered tens of thousands of casualties and had more than sixty thousand soldiers captured, the United States and its allies lost fewer than 150 troops and had only forty-one prisoners taken by Iraqi forces.

One of the reasons war shows the Law of Timing so clearly is that the consequences are so dramatic and immediate. If you look back at any major battle, you'll be able to see the critical importance of timing. The Battle of Gettysburg during the American Civil War is a prime example.

The stage was set for the conflict when Confederate General Robert E. Lee took the Army of Northern Virginia into Pennsylvania in late June of 1863. It was the third year of the war, and both nations were growing weary of the conflict. Lee's actions had three goals: (1) draw the Union army out of Virginia, (2) resupply his troops using Pennsylvania's resources, and (3) bring the fighting to the heart of enemy territory, hoping to thereby precipitate an end to the conflict.

The general's strategy was to move on Harrisburg, Pennsylvania, in an attempt to prod the Union army—last known to be in Virginia— into a hasty and unwanted action. Several days prior to the battle, Lee told General Trimble,

> Our army is in good spirits, not overfatigued, and can be concentrated on any one point in twenty-four hours or less. I have not yet heard that the enemy have crossed the Potomac, and am waiting to hear from General Stuart. When they hear where we are, they will make forced marches . . . They will come up . . . broken down from hunger and hard marching, strung out on a long line and much demoralized, when they come into Pennsylvania. I shall throw an overwhelming force on their advance, crush it, follow up the success, drive one corps back on another, and by successive repulses and surprises, before they can concentrate, create a panic and virtually destroy the army.[4]

Lee was trying to seize the opportunity for overwhelming victory. He didn't know until the morning of July 1 that the Union army had already moved north. By then some of its forces were already engaging Confederate troops on the Chambersburg Road west of Gettysburg. That development disrupted Lee's strategy and ruined his timing.

Lee's first instinct was to hold back and wait for his army's full strength to assemble before forcing a major engagement. But always conscious of the Law of Timing, he recognized when his troops had a sudden advantage. As Lee watched from a nearby ridge, he saw that Federal troops were being routed and retreating. Confederate forces had an opportunity to seize the high ground of Cemetery Hill, defended only by a few Union infantry reserves and artillery. If they could capture and control that position, Lee reasoned, they would control the whole area. It would be the key to a Confederate victory and possibly bring an end to the war.

TIMING MISSED, OPPORTUNITY GONE

But the South did not secure that hill. Though it was still early in the day and the time was ripe to execute an effective attack, Confederate General R. S. Ewell, who was in position to take the hill, simply watched instead of engaging the enemy. And the opportunity slipped away. By the next morning, Union troops had reinforced their previous positions, and the South's chance was gone. The Northern and Southern armies fought for two more days, but in the end, Lee's forces suffered defeat, having lost about 33,000 of his 76,300 men to injury or death.[5] Their only choice was to retreat and make their way back to Virginia.

ANOTHER OPPORTUNITY LOST

After the South's defeat, Lee expected the Union forces under the leadership of General Meade to immediately pursue a counterattack and utterly destroy his reeling army. That was also the expectation of

Abraham Lincoln after he received the news of the Union's victory. Anxious to make the most of the Law of Timing, Lincoln sent a communication from Washington, D.C., to Meade via General Halleck on July 7, 1863. In it, Halleck said,

> I have received from the President the following note, which I respectfully communicate.
>
> "We have certain information that Vicksburg surrendered to General Grant on the 4th of July. Now, if General Meade can complete his work so gloriously prosecuted thus far by the literal or substantial destruction of Lee's army, the rebellion will be over."[6]

Lincoln recognized that the timing was right for an action that could end the war. But just as the Southern forces did not seize the moment for victory when it was available, neither did their Northern counterparts. Meade took his time following up his victory at Gettysburg, and he didn't pursue Lee aggressively enough. When he announced his goal, saying he would "drive from our soil every vestige of the presence of the invader," Lincoln's response was, "My God, is that all?" Lincoln knew he was seeing the Union's chance slip away.

The Law of Timing had been violated. On July 14, what remained of the Army of Northern Virginia crossed over the Potomac, escaping destruction. Lincoln was appalled that the Union had missed a chance to end the war. Later he said that Meade's efforts had reminded him of "an old woman trying to shoo her geese across a creek."[7]

In the end, both armies had missed their best opportunity to achieve victory. Instead, the fighting continued for almost two more years, and hundreds of thousands more troops died. Leaders from both sides had known what to do to achieve victory, but they failed to follow through at the critical moment.

Reading a situation and knowing what to do are not enough to make you succeed in leadership. Only the right action *at the right time* will bring success. Anything else exacts a high price. That's the Law of Timing.

20

THE LAW OF EXPLOSIVE GROWTH

To Add Growth, Lead Followers—
To Multiply, Lead Leaders

IN 1984 AT AGE TWENTY-TWO, John Schnatter started his own business. He began by selling pizzas out of a converted broom closet at Mick's Tavern, a lounge that was co-owned by his father. Although he was just a kid, he had a tremendous amount of vision, drive, and energy—enough to make his tiny pizza stand into a success. The next year, he opened his first store next door to Mick's in Jeffersonville, Indiana. He named the place Papa John's. For the next several years, Schnatter worked hard to build the company. In time, he opened additional stores, and later he began selling franchises. By the beginning of 1991, he had 46 stores. That in itself is a success story. But what happened during the next couple of years is even better.

In 1991 and 1992, Papa John's turned a huge corner. By the end of 1991, the number of stores more than doubled to 110 units. By the end of 1992, they had doubled again to 220. And the growth has continued dramatically. In early 1998, that number surpassed 1,600. What made the company suddenly experience such an incredible period of rapid expansion? The answer can be found in the Law of Explosive Growth.

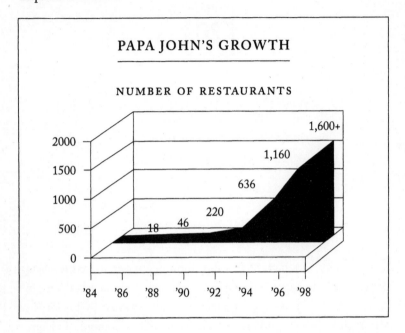

Schnatter had always hired good people for his staff, but in the early years he was really the sole leader and primary driving force behind the business's success. Back in the 1980s, he didn't dedicate much time to developing other strong leaders. "It's taking a lot of growing on my part," says Schnatter of Papa John's success. "Between

> "It's my job to build the people who are going to build the company."
> —John Schnatter

26 and 32 [years old], the hardest thing was I had a lot of John Schnatters around me [people with great potential who needed to be mentored]. They needed a lot of coaching, and I was so busy developing myself, trying to get myself to the next level, I didn't develop those people. As a result, I lost them. It's my job to build the people who are going to build

the company. That's going to be much harder for me than the first 1,200 stores."[1]

THE KEY TO GROWTH IS LEADERSHIP

In the early 1990s, Schnatter began thinking about what it would take to really grow the company. The key was leadership. He had already begun to grow as a leader personally. His having made significant progress in his leadership development was opening the door for him to attract better leaders to the company and to give them the time they needed. That's when he started recruiting some of the people who currently lead the company, including Wade Oney, now the company's chief operating officer. Wade had worked for Domino's Pizza for fourteen years, and John believed he was one of the reasons that company had been so successful. When Wade left Domino's, John immediately asked him to be a part of the Papa John's Pizza team.

Schnatter had already built a company capable of creating a taste-tempting pizza—and earning a healthy profit in the process. (Their per store sales average is higher than that of Pizza Hut, Domino's, or Little Caesar's.) Their goal was to build a bigger company. Together, they started talking about what it would take to be capable of opening four hundred to five hundred new restaurants a year. And that's when they focused their attention on developing leaders so that they could take the company to the next level. Says Oney, "The reason we're successful in the marketplace is our focus on quality and our desire to keep things simple. The reason we're successful as a company is our good people."

Since the early 1990s, Schnatter and Oney have developed a top-rate team of leaders who are helping the company experience explosive growth, people such as Blaine Hurst, Papa John's president and vice chairman; Drucilla "Dru" Milby, the CFO; Robert Waddell, president of Papa John's Food Service; and Hart Boesel, who heads up franchise operations.

Papa John's growth has been phenomenal in an industry that was thought to be glutted with competitors a decade ago. In 1997, they opened more than 350 new restaurants. In 1998, they expect the number to be more than 400. And they are also implementing plans to launch Papa John's internationally. They don't plan to stop growing until they are the largest seller of pizza in the world.

"The challenge now," explains Oney, "is developing the next leaders. The company's in great shape financially. [Acquiring] real estate is always a battle, but we can succeed there. And the economy is never a deterrent when you offer customers a good value. The key is to develop leaders. You do that by building up people."

LEADER'S MATH BRINGS EXPLOSIVE GROWTH

John Schnatter and Wade Oney have succeeded because they have practiced the Law of Explosive Growth. Any leader who does that makes the shift from follower's math to what I call leader's math.

> *Any leader who practices the Law of Explosive Growth makes the shift from follower's math to leader's math.*

Here's how it works. Leaders who develop followers grow their organization only one person at a time. But leaders who develop leaders multiply their growth, because for every leader they develop, they also receive all of that leader's followers. Add ten followers to your organization, and you have the power of ten people. Add ten leaders to your organization, and you have the power of ten leaders times all the followers and leaders *they* influence. That's the difference between addition and multiplication. It's like growing your organization by teams instead of by individuals. The better the leaders you develop, the greater the quality and quantity of followers.

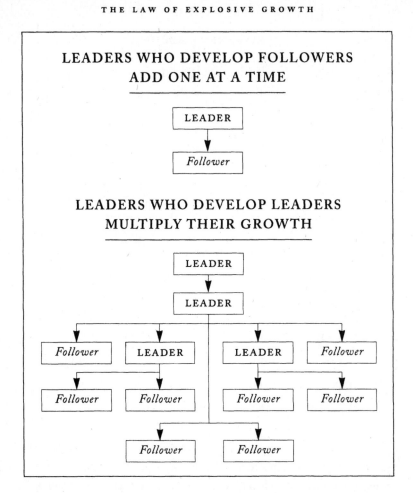

To go to the highest level, you have to develop leaders of leaders. My friend Dale Galloway asserts that "some leaders want to make followers. I want to make leaders. Not only do I want to make leaders, but I want to make leaders of leaders. And then leaders of leaders of leaders." Once you are able to follow that pattern, there is almost no limit to the growth of your organization. That's why I say to add growth, lead followers, but to muliply growth, lead leaders. That's the Law of Explosive Growth.

A DIFFERENT FOCUS

Becoming a leader who develops leaders requires an entirely different focus and attitude from those of a developer of followers. Consider some of the differences:

LEADERS WHO DEVELOP FOLLOWERS	LEADERS WHO DEVELOP LEADERS
Need to be needed	Want to be succeeded
Focus on weaknesses	Focus on strengths
Develop the bottom 20 percent	Develop the top 20 percent
Treat their people the same for "fairness"	Treat their leaders as individuals for impact
Hoard power	Give power away
Spend time with others	Invest time in others
Grow by addition	Grow by multiplication
Impact only people they touch personally	Impact people far beyond their own reach

Developing leaders is difficult because potential leaders are harder to find and attract. They're also harder to hold on to once you find them because unlike followers, they are energetic and entrepreneurial, and they tend to want to go their own way. Developing leaders is also hard work. Leadership development isn't an add-water-and-stir proposition. It takes time, energy, and resources.

A LEADER DEVELOPED FROM AFAR

I've made the development of leaders my focus in life for the last twenty years. The impact on my organizations has always been very rewarding. But in the last ten years, I've also had the incredible privilege of seeing it impact other leaders and their organizations. That's happened because many of the leaders I've helped develop over the last decade work in organizations other than my own. As a result, I'm occasionally surprised to find someone I've developed without even knowing it. That's what happened when I held a conference overseas last fall.

As I mentioned in previous chapters, I sometimes teach leadership outside the United States. Over the years, I've held conferences in Australia, Brazil, Canada, India, Indonesia, Korea, New Zealand, Nigeria, and South Africa. In addition, my books have been translated into more than twenty languages, and my tapes are distributed to countries all over the globe. So I know my leadership principles have traveled far. But I was still pleasantly surprised when I traveled to India last fall, met David Mohan for the first time in the city of Madras, and heard his remarkable story.

Pastor Mohan leads the largest Christian church in all of India. I traveled there to teach leadership to a group of about two thousand pastors. When I arrived, he greeted me like a long-lost friend. I was running late that morning, our plane having been delayed five hours prior to our arrival, so he and I didn't have much time to talk before the conference began. As I taught leadership, he sat on the front row soaking up everything I said. When I taught the Law of Priorities and the Pareto Principle, I saw that he gathered his top leaders around him to make sure they understood all that I was communicating. And occasionally, as I introduced another principle that is part of my foundational teachings on leadership, he seemed to anticipate what I was about to say.

When we finished the conference, he warmly thanked me and insisted on driving me to the airport. As we made the long drive, he told me his story. He said that he was originally scheduled to be in Pittsburgh, Pennsylvania, during this conference, but when he heard that I was coming, he changed his plans because he wanted to meet me. Seven years earlier, his church had been comprised of about seven hundred people. That is a good-sized church, especially in India. But he wanted to reach more people and make a greater impact on his area. And he recognized that to do it, he needed to start developing leaders among his people.

Around that time, someone told him about my books and tapes on leadership. For the next seven years, he was like a sponge, reading my books, listening to my tapes, and soaking up everything he could learn about leadership. And he was also developing people into strong leaders. As he grew, so did his team of leaders. As they grew, so did his church. By the time I visited in the fall of 1997,

> *The only way to experience an explosive level of growth is to do the math—leader's math.*

fourteen thousand people were attending the church's services every weekend. Not only that, but one out of every ten people in his church has been trained and developed as a leader. And he was thanking *me* for help I'd unknowingly given him.

I felt humbled by what he told me; I also felt incredibly encouraged. I started wondering how many other men and women were out there that I had never met who had learned about leadership and were making a greater impact on people as a result. Meeting him and hearing his story underlined my commitment to continue teaching leadership.

I don't know where you are in your journey of leadership development. You may be working on your leadership growth, or you may already be a highly developed leader. No matter where you are, I know one thing: You will go to the highest level only if you begin developing leaders instead of followers. Leaders who develop leaders experience an incredible multiplication effect in their organizations that can be achieved in no other way—not by increasing resources, reducing costs, increasing profit margins, analyzing systems, implementing quality management procedures, or doing anything else. The only way to experience an explosive level of growth is to do the math—leader's math. That's the incredible power of the Law of Explosive Growth.

THE LAW OF LEGACY

A Leader's Lasting Value Is
Measured by Succession

I N 1997, ONE OF the finest business leaders in the world died. His name was Roberto Goizueta, and he was the chairman and chief executive of the Coca-Cola Company. In a speech he gave to the Executives' Club of Chicago a few months before he died, Goizueta made this statement: "A billion hours ago, human life appeared on Earth. A billion minutes ago, Christianity emerged. A billion seconds ago, the Beatles performed on 'The Ed Sullivan Show.' A billion Coca-Colas ago . . . was yesterday morning. And the question we are asking ourselves now is, 'What must we do to make a billion Coca-Colas ago this morning?'"

Making Coca-Cola the best company in the world was Goizueta's lifelong quest, one he was still pursuing diligently when he suddenly, unexpectedly died. Companies that lose a CEO often go into turmoil, especially if his departure is unexpected, as Goizueta's was. Shortly before his death, Goizueta said in an interview with the *Atlanta Journal-Constitution* that retirement was "not on my radar screen. As long as I'm having the fun I'm having, as long as I have the energy necessary, as long as I'm not keeping people from their day in the sun, and as long as the board wants me to stay on, I will stay on." Just months after the interview, he was diagnosed with cancer. Six weeks later, he was dead.

Upon Goizueta's death, former president Jimmy Carter observed, "Perhaps no other corporate leader in modern times has so beautifully exemplified the American dream. He believed that in America, all things are possible. He lived that dream. And because of his extraordinary leadership skills, he helped thousands of others realize their dreams as well."

GOIZUETA'S LEGACY

The legacy left to the company by Goizueta is incredible. When he took over Coca-Cola in 1981, the company's value was $4 billion. Under Goizueta's leadership, it rose to $150 billion. That's an increase in value of more than 3,500 percent! Coca-Cola became the second most valuable corporation in America, ahead of the car makers, the oil companies, Microsoft, Wal-Mart, and all the rest. The only company more valuable was General Electric. Many of Coke's stockholders became millionaires many times over. Emory University in Atlanta, whose portfolio contains a large block of Coca-Cola stock, now has an endowment comparable to that of Harvard.

But high stock value wasn't the most significant thing Goizueta gave to the Coca-Cola company. Instead it was the way he lived the Law of Legacy. When the CEO's death was announced, there was no panic among Coca-Cola stockholders. Paine Webber analyst Emanuel Goldman said that Goizueta "prepared the company for his not being there as well as any executive I've ever seen."

How did he do it? First, by making the company as strong as he possibly could. Second, by preparing a successor for the top position named Douglas Ivester. Mickey H. Gramig, writer for the *Atlanta*

Constitution, reported, "Unlike some companies, which face a crisis when the top executive leaves or dies, Coca-Cola is expected to retain its status as one of the world's most admired corporations. Goizueta had groomed Ivester to follow his footsteps since the Georgia native's 1994 appointment to the company's No. 2 post. And as an indication of how strongly Wall Street felt about Coca-Cola's footings, the company's stock barely rippled six weeks ago when Goizueta was diagnosed with lung cancer."[1]

Doug Ivester, an accountant by training, started his career with Coca-Cola in 1979 as the assistant controller. Four years later, he was named chief financial officer. He was known for his exceptional financial creativity, and he was a major force in Goizueta's ability to revolutionize the company's approach to investment and the handling of debt. By 1989, Goizueta must have decided that Ivester had untapped potential, because he moved him out of his strictly financial role and sent him to Europe to obtain operating and international experience. A year later, Goizueta brought him back and named him president of Coca-Cola USA, where he oversaw expenditures and marketing. From there he continued to groom Ivester, and in 1994, there could be no doubt that Ivester would follow Goizueta into the top position. Goizueta made him president and chief operating officer.

What Roberto Goizueta did was very unusual. Few chief executives of companies today develop strong leaders and groom them to take over the organization. John S. Wood, a consultant at Egon Zehnder International Inc., has noted that "companies have not in the recent past been investing as heavily in bringing people up. If they're not able to grow them, they have to go get them." So why was Roberto Goizueta different? He was a product of the Law of Legacy.

Roberto Goizueta was born in Cuba and educated at Yale, where he earned a degree in chemical engineering. When he returned to Havana in 1954, he answered a newspaper ad for a bilingual chemist.

The company hiring turned out to be Coca-Cola. By 1966, he had become vice president of technical research and development at the company's headquarters in Atlanta. He was the youngest man ever to hold such a position in the company. But in the early 1970s, something even more important happened. Robert W. Woodruff, the patriarch of Coca-Cola, took Goizueta under his wing and began developing him. In 1975, Goizueta became the executive vice president of the company's technical division and took on other corporate responsibilities, such as overseeing legal affairs. And in 1980, with Woodruff's blessing, Goizueta became president and chief operating officer. One year later he was the chairman and chief executive. The reason Goizueta so confidently selected, developed, and groomed a successor in the 1990s is that he was building on the legacy that he had received in the 1970s.

> *"Leadership is one of the things you cannot delegate. You either exercise it, or you abdicate it."*
> —*Robert Goizueta*

LEADERS WHO LEAVE
A LEGACY OF SUCCESSION . . .

Goizueta once said, "Leadership is one of the things you cannot delegate. You either exercise it, or you abdicate it." I believe there is a third choice: You pass it on to your successor. That's a choice Goizueta exercised. Leaders who practice the Law of Legacy are rare. But the ones who do leave a legacy of succession for their organization by doing the following:

LEAD THE ORGANIZATION WITH A "LONG VIEW"

Just about anybody can make an organization look good for a moment—by launching a flashy new program or product, drawing crowds to a big event, or slashing the budget to boost the bottom line. But leaders who leave a legacy take a different approach. They lead with tomorrow as well as today in mind. That's what Goizueta did. He planned to keep leading as long as he was effective, yet he prepared his successor anyway. He always looked out for the best interests of the organization and its stockholders.

> *Just as in sports a coach needs a team of good players to win, an organization needs a team of good leaders to succeed.*

CREATE A LEADERSHIP CULTURE

The most stable companies have strong leaders at every level of the organization. The only way to develop such widespread leadership is to make developing leaders a part of your culture. That is a strong part of Coca-Cola's legacy. How many other successful companies do you know about that have had a succession of leaders come up within the ranks of their own organization?

PAY THE PRICE TODAY TO ASSURE SUCCESS TOMORROW

There is no success without sacrifice. Each organization is unique, and that dictates what the price will be. But any leader who wants to help his organization must be willing to pay that price to ensure lasting success.

VALUE TEAM LEADERSHIP ABOVE INDIVIDUAL LEADERSHIP

No matter how good he is, no leader can do it all alone. Just as in sports a coach needs a team of good players to win, an organization needs a team of good *leaders* to succeed. The larger the organization, the stronger, larger, and deeper the team of leaders needs to be.

WALK AWAY FROM THE ORGANIZATION WITH INTEGRITY

In the case of Coca-Cola, the leader didn't get the opportunity to walk away because he died an untimely death. But if he had lived, I believe Goizueta would have done just that. When it's a leader's time to leave the organization, he has got to be willing to walk away and let his successor do his own thing. Meddling only hurts him and the organization.

A LEGACY OF SUCCESSION

I mentioned in the chapter on the Law of Buy-In that in the fall of 1997, I went to India with a handful of leaders from my nonprofit organization EQUIP. While we were there, I wanted to visit the headquarters of Mother Teresa. It's a plain concrete block building located in Calcutta, which the people there call the Mother House.

As I stood outside the doors preparing to go in, I thought about how no one could tell by looking at it that this modest place had been the home base of such an effective leader. We walked through a foyer and into a central patio that was open to the sky. Our goal was to visit Mother Teresa's tomb, which is located in the facility's dining room. But when we got there, we found out that the room was in use and we would not be allowed to go in until the ceremony that was being performed was over.

We could see a group of about forty to fifty nuns seated, all dressed in the familiar habit that Mother Teresa had worn.

"What's going on in there?" I asked a nun passing by.

She smiled. "Today we are taking forty-five new members into our order," she said and then hurried away into another part of the building.

Since we were already running late and soon had to catch a plane, we couldn't stay. We looked around briefly and then left. As I walked out of the compound, through an alley, and out among the throngs of people, I thought to myself, *Mother Teresa would have been proud.* She was gone, but her legacy was continuing. She had made an impact on the world, and she had developed leaders who were carrying on her vision. And it looks as though they will continue influencing people for generations to come. Mother Teresa's life is a great example of the Law of Legacy.

FEW LEADERS PASS IT ON

Max Dupree, author of *Leadership Is an Art*, declared, "Succession is one of the key responsibilities of leadership." Yet of all the laws of leadership, the Law of Legacy is the one that the fewest leaders seem to learn. Achievement comes to someone when he is able to do great things for himself. Success comes when he empowers followers to do great things *with* him. Significance comes when he develops leaders to do great things *for* him. But a legacy is created only when a person puts his organization into the position to do great things *without* him.

> *A legacy is created only when a person puts his organization into the position to do great things without him.*

I learned the Law of Legacy the hard way. Because the church grew so much while I was in my first leadership position in Hillham, Indiana, I thought I was a success. When I began there, we had only three people in attendance. For three years, I built up that church, reached out to the community, and influenced many people's lives. When I left, our average attendance was in the high two hundreds, and our record was more than three hundred people. I had programs in place, and everything looked rosy to me. I thought I had really done something significant.

When I had been at my second church for about eighteen months, I had lunch with a friend I hadn't seen in a while, and he had just spent some time in Hillham. I asked him about how things were going back there, and I was surprised to hear his answer.

"Not too good," he answered.

"Really?" I said. "Why? Things were going great when I left. What's wrong?"

"Well," he said, "it's kind of fallen off. Some of the programs you got started kind of petered out. The church is running only about a hundred people. It might get even smaller before it's all over."

That really bothered me. A leader hates to see something that he put his sweat, blood, and tears into starting to fail. At first, I got ticked off at the leader who followed me. But then it hit me. If I had done a really good job there, it wouldn't matter what kind of leader followed me, good or bad. The fault was really mine. I hadn't set up the organization to succeed after I left. It was the first time I realized the significance of the Law of Legacy.

PARADIGM SHIFT

After that, I started to look at leadership in a whole new way. Every leader eventually leaves his organization—one way or another. He may change jobs, get promoted, or retire. And even if a person refuses to retire, he is going to die. That made me realize that part of my job as a leader was to start preparing my people and organization for what inevitably lies ahead. That prompted me to change my focus from leading followers to developing leaders. My lasting value, like that of any leader, would be measured by my ability to give the organization a smooth succession.

My best personal succession story concerns my departure from Skyline Church. When I first arrived there in 1981, I made one of my primary goals the identification and development of leaders because I knew that our success depended on it. Over the fourteen years I was there, my staff and I developed literally hundreds of outstanding leaders, both volunteers and staff.

The development of so many leaders put the church in a good position to succeed, but that alone wasn't enough. In many businesses and nonprofit organizations, the leader is in a position to develop and groom a successor. That wasn't something I was able to do at Skyline.

The local board of administration would select someone to succeed me, and I would not drive that process. The most I would be able to do was give them any information I knew about the potential candidates with whom I was acquainted. But there were other things I *could* do, such as preparing the people and the organization for the arrival of their new leader. I wanted to set that person up to succeed as much as I could.

THE SUCCESS CONTINUES

One of my greatest joys in life is knowing that Skyline is stronger now than when I left in 1995. Jim Garlow, who succeeded me as the senior pastor, is doing a wonderful job there. The church's attendance has increased, finances have improved, and best of all, the building and relocation program is going forward after a decade of delays. In the fall of 1997, Jim asked me to come back to Skyline and speak at a fund-raising banquet for the next phase of the building project, and I was delighted to honor his request.

They staged the event at the San Diego Convention Center, located on the city's beautiful bay. They really did a first-class job of everything, and about 4,100 people attended. My wife, Margaret, and I really enjoyed the chance to see and talk with so many of our old friends. And of course, I felt privileged to be the evening's keynote speaker. It was quite a celebration—and quite a success. People pledged more than $7.8 million toward the building of the church's new facility.

As soon as I finished speaking, Margaret and I slipped out of the ballroom. We wanted the night to belong to Jim, since he was now the leader of Skyline. Because of that, we knew it would be best if we made a quick exit before the program was over. Descending the stairs, I grabbed her hand and gave it a squeeze.

"Margaret," I said, "wasn't it an awesome night?"

"Oh, it was great," she said. "I think Jim was really pleased."

"I think you're right," I said. "You know what was the best part for me? Knowing that what we started all those years ago is going to continue." As we left the convention center behind us, I felt that our final chapter with Skyline was finished, and it had a very happy ending. It's like my friend Chris Musgrove says, "Success is not measured by what you're leaving to, but by what you are leaving behind."

When all is said and done, your ability as a leader will not be judged by what you achieved personally or even by what your team accomplished during your tenure. You will be judged by how well your people and your organization did after you were gone. You will be gauged according to the Law of Legacy. Your lasting value will be measured by succession.

CONCLUSION

*Everything Rises and
Falls on Leadership*

WELL, THERE YOU have them—the 21 Irrefutable Laws of Leadership. Learn them, take them to heart, and apply them to your life. If you follow them, people will follow you.

I've been teaching leadership for two and a half decades now, and during those years I've told the people I've trained something that I'm now going to say to you: Everything rises and falls on leadership. Most people don't believe me when I say that, but it's true. The more you try to do in life, the more you will find that leadership makes the difference. Any endeavor you can undertake that involves other people will live or die depending on leadership. As you work to build your organization, remember this:

- Personnel determine the potential of the organization.
- Relationships determine the morale of the organization.
- Structure determines the size of the organization.
- Vision determines the direction of the organization.
- Leadership determines the success of the organization.

I wish you success. Pursue your dreams. Desire excellence. Become the person you were created to be. And accomplish all that you were put on this earth to do. Leadership will help you to do that. Learn to lead—not just for yourself, but for the people who follow behind you. And as you reach the highest levels, don't forget to take others with you to be the leaders of tomorrow.

NOTES

CHAPTER 1

1. John F. Love, *McDonald's: Behind the Arches* (New York: Bantam Books, 1986).

CHAPTER 2

1. Quoted at www.abcnews.com on 4 February 1998.
2. Thomas A. Stewart, "Brain Power: Who Owns It . . . How They Profit from It," *Fortune,* 17 March 1997, 105–6.
3. Paul F. Boller, Jr., *Presidential Anecdotes* (New York: Penguin Books, 1981), 129.

CHAPTER 3

1. Sharon E. Epperson, "Death and the Maven," *Time,* 18 December 1995.
2. James K. Glassman, "An Old Lady's Lesson: Patience Usually Pays," *Washington Post,* 17 December 1995, H01.
3. "The Champ," *Reader's Digest,* January 1972, 109.
4. Milton Meltzer, *Theodore Roosevelt and His America* (New York: Franklin Watts, 1994).

CHAPTER 4

1. *Forbes.*

CHAPTER 5

1. Bruce Nash and Allan Zullo, *The Sports Hall of Shame.*
2. Peggy Noonan, *Time* 15 September 1997.

CHAPTER 6

1. E. M. Swift, "Odd Man Out," *Sports Illustrated,* 92–96.
2. Robert Shaw, "Tough Trust," *Leader to Leader* (winter 1997), 46–54.
3. Russell Duncan, *Blue-Eyed Child of Fortune* (Athens: University of Georgia Press, 1992), 52–54.
4. Robert S. McNamara with Brian VanDeMark, *In Retrospect: The Tragedy and Lessons of Vietnam* (New York: Times Books, 1995).

CHAPTER 7

1. M. W. Taylor, *Harriet Tubman* (New York: Chelsea House Publishers, 1991).
2. Alexander Wolff, "Tales Out of School," *Sports Illustrated,* 20 October 1997, 64.
3. Mitchell Krugel, *Jordan: The Man, His Words, His Life* (New York: St. Martin's Press, 1994), 39.

CHAPTER 8

1. Cathy Booth, "Steve's Job: Restart Apple," *Time,* 18 August 1997, 28–34.
2. Michael Krantz, "If You Can't Beat 'Em," *Time,* 18 August 1997, 35–37.

CHAPTER 10

1. Quoted in Atlanta *Journal-Constitution,* 9 January 1998.
2. H. Norman Schwarzkopf, "Lessons in Leadership," Vol. 12, no. 5.
3. H. Norman Schwarzkopf and Peter Petre, *It Doesn't Take a Hero* (New York: Bantam Books, 1992).
4. Kevin and Jackie Freiberg, *Nuts! Southwest Airlines' Crazy Recipe for Business* (New York: Broadway Books, 1996), 224.

CHAPTER 11

1. Lawrence Miller, *American Spirit: Visions of a New Corporate Culture.*

2. Warren Bennis, *Scarce Organizing Genius: The Secrets of Creative Collaboration.*
3. Judith M. Bardwick, *In Praise of Good Business* (New York: John Wiley and Sons, 1988).
4. Prov. 27:17 CEV.

CHAPTER 12

1. Peter Collier and David Horowitz, *The Fords: An American Epic* (New York: Summit Books, 1987).
2. Lee Iacocca and William Novak, *Iacocca: An Autobiography* (New York: Bantam Books, 1984).
3. Lynne Joy McFarland, John R. Childress, and Larry E. Senn, *21st Century Leadership: Dialogues with 100 Top Leaders* (Leadership Press, 1993).
4. Benjamin P. Thomas, *Abraham Lincoln: A Biography* (New York: Modern Library, 1968), 235.
5. Richard Wheeler, *Witness to Gettysburg* (New York: Harper and Row, 1987).
6. Donald T. Phillips, *Lincoln on Leadership: Executive Strategies for Tough Times* (New York: Warner Books, 1992), 103–4.

CHAPTER 13

1. Janet Lowe, *Jack Welch Speaks: Wisdom from the World's Greatest Business Leader* (New York: John Wiley and Sons, 1998).

CHAPTER 14

1. Otis Port, "Love Among the Digerati," *Business Week*, 25 August 1997, 102.

CHAPTER 15

1. David M. Potter, *Jefferson Davis and the Political Factors in Confederate Defeat.*

2. James C. Humes, *The Wit and Wisdom of Winston Churchill* (New York: Harper Perennial, 1994).
3. Arthur Schlesinger Jr., "Franklin Delano Roosevelt," *Time,* 13 April 1998.
4. Andre Brink, "Nelson Mandela," *Time,* 13 April 1998.
5. Mitchell Krugel, *Jordan: The Man, His Words, His Life* (New York: St. Martin's Press, 1994), 41.
6. Kevin and Jackie Freiberg, *Nuts! Southwest Airlines' Crazy Recipe for Business and Personal Success* (New York: Broadway Books, 1996).

CHAPTER 16

1. Jay Mathews, *Escalante: The Best Teacher in America* (New York: Henry Holt, 1988).

CHAPTER 17

1. John Wooden and Jack Tobin, *They Call Me Coach* (Chicago: Contemporary Books, 1988).
2. Janet C. Lowe, *Jack Welch Speaks: Wisdom from the World's Greatest Business Leader* (New York: John Wiley and Sons, 1998).

CHAPTER 18

1. Lee Iacocca and William Novak, *Iacocca: An Autobiography* (New York: Bantam Books, 1984).
2. Hillary Margolis, "A Whole New Set of Glitches for Digital's Robert Palmer," *Fortune,* 19 August 1996, 193–94.
3. David Wallechinsky, *The Twentieth Century* (Boston: Little, Brown, 1995), 155.

CHAPTER 19

1. Paul F. Boller Jr., *Presidential Anecdotes* (New York: Penguin Books, 1981), 340.
2. Peter G. Bourne, *Jimmy Carter: A Comprehensive Biography from Plains to Postpresidency* (New York: Scribner, 1997).

3. Daniel B. Baker, *Power Quotes* (Detroit: Visible Ink Press, 1992), 337.

4. Douglas Southall Freeman, *Lee: An Abridgement in One Volume* (New York: Charles Scribner's Sons, 1961), 319.

5. Samuel P. Bates, *The Battle of Gettysburg* (Philadelphia: T. H. Davis and Company, 1875), 198–99.

6. Ibid.

7. Richard Wheeler, *Witness to Gettysburg* (New York: Harper and Row, 1987).

CHAPTER 20

1. Rajan Chaudhry, "Dough Boy," *Chain Leader*, April 1997.

CHAPTER 21

1. Mickey H. Gramig, *Atlanta Constitution*, 10 November 1997.

STEP UP

TO THE

21 LAWS OF LEADERSHIP!

STEP 1 Assess Your Leadership Strengths

You can take your leadership to the next level, and Maximum Impact® will help you every step of the way! Begin your own leadership challenge at www.maximumimpact.com/4steps. The *21 Laws* leadership assessment will tell you where you are as a leader today and will guide you to where you need to be tomorrow.

> **Visit www.maximumimpact.com/4steps and take your FREE assessment!**

STEP 2 Begin Your Leadership Training

Log on to www.maximumimpact.com/4steps and receive a free copy of *Leadership Aptitudes*. This lesson was specifically chosen from John C. Maxwell's Maximum Impact Club series to help you take the next step in your leadership training! *Leadership Aptitudes* is available to you either online in streaming audio format or, if you would prefer to add this lesson to your personal leadership training library, we can ship you a copy on either audiocassette or CD for a minimal shipping charge of $2.00.

> **Visit www.maximumimpact.com/4steps and download your FREE audio lesson! Available online or on audiocassette/CD.**

STEP 3 Train with the Best Resources

If you're going to be the best, you've got to train with the best! Purchase the complete audio (for your personal use) and video (for group training) *21 Laws* series and maximize your leadership potential!

Living the 21 Irrefutable Laws of Leadership
Audio Curriculum by John C. Maxwell

You will achieve more than you ever imagined by simply listening to one leadership lesson, reading one chapter, and completing one assignment each month. With *Living the 21 Laws,* you'll have a leadership growth tool that will allow you to:

- **Evaluate your leadership strengths**
- **Create a proactive plan to improve your leadership skills**
- **Understand the laws so that you can readily teach them**

Learning the 21 Irrefutable Laws of Leadership
Video Curriculum by John C. Maxwell

How do you propel your organization to a new level? Make sure that you are all growing together! These dynamic videos will allow you to bring your entire leadership team together to develop a shared vision, a corporate purpose, and a unified effort. Plus, it will make teaching easier and less time-consuming for you.

STEP 4 Train with a Proven Coach

Let John C. Maxwell mentor you monthly!

Maximum Impact®: The Monthly Mentoring Leadership Club for Marketplace Leaders
Audio Program
(Available on CD or Audiocassette)

Most leaders will agree that regardless of how long they've been in a leadership position, there are issues they face every day where they would like some insight and helpful perspective. John will provide you with such mentorship on a monthly basis.

Order these resources at www.maximumimpact.com.

Books by Dr. John C. Maxwell
Can Teach You How to Be a REAL Success

RELATIONSHIPS

Be a People Person (Victor Books)
Becoming a Person of Influence (Thomas Nelson)
The Treasure of a Friend (J. Countryman)

EQUIPPING

Developing the Leaders Around You (Thomas Nelson)
Success One Day at a Time (J. Countryman)

ATTITUDE

Failing Forward (Thomas Nelson)
Living at the Next Level (Thomas Nelson)
The Winning Attitude (Thomas Nelson)
The Power of Attitude (Honor Books)
Your Road Map for Success (Thomas Nelson)

LEADERSHIP

Developing the Leader Within You (Thomas Nelson)
Leadership 101 (Thomas Nelson)
Leading from the Lockers (Tommy Nelson)
The Maxwell Leadership Bible (Thomas Nelson)
The Power of Leadership (Honor Books)
The 17 Essential Qualities of a Team Player (Thomas Nelson)
The 17 Indisputable Laws of Teamwork (Thomas Nelson)
The 21 Indispensable Qualities of a Leader (Thomas Nelson)
The 21 Most Powerful Minutes in a Leader's Day (Thomas Nelson)